COWLEY PUBLICATIONS is a ministry of the brothers of the Society of Saint John the Evangelist, a monastic order in the Episcopal Church. Our mission is to provide books and resources for those seeking spiritual and theological formation. COWLEY PUBLICATIONS is committed to developing a new generation of writers and teachers who will encourage people to think and pray in new ways about spirituality, reconciliation, and the future.

T0159023

⇛ HARBORS OF HEAVEN

HARBORS OF HEAVEN

Bethlehem and the Places We Love

Jeffrey Johnson

Cowley Publications

CAMBRIDGE, MASSACHUSETTS

Published in the United States of America by Cowley Publications, a division of the Society of Saint John the Evangelist. No portion of this book may be reproduced, stored in or introduced into a retrieval system, or transmitted, in any form or by any means— including photocopying—without the prior written permission of Cowley Publications, except in the case of brief quotations embedded in critical articles and reviews.

Library of Congress Cataloging-in-Publication Data

Johnson, Jeffrey, 1959–
    Harbors of heaven : Bethlehem and the places we love / Jeffrey Johnson.
        p.   cm.
    Includes bibliographical references.
    ISBN-10: 1-56101-267-X   ISBN-13: 978-1-56101-267-1 (pbk. : alk. paper)
    1. Jesus Christ—Nativity.   2. Religion and geography.   I. Title.
    BT315.3.J64 2006
    232.92—dc22

                                    2005023466

Scripture quotations are taken from The New Revised Standard Version of the Bible, © 1989, by the Division of Christian Education of the National Council of the Churches of Christ in the United States of America. Used by permission.

"Anecdote of a Jar" and "A Rabbit as King of the Ghosts" from *The Collected Poems of Wallace Stevens* by Wallace Stevens, copyright 1954 by Wallace Stevens and renewed 1982 by Holly Stevens. Used by permission of Alfred A. Knopf, a division of Random House, Inc.

"Carol of Brother Ass," "Lullaby after Sleeping," "Old Dog," and "Homecoming Blues" by Vassar Miller are used by permission of Southern Methodist University Press.

"The Gift" by William Carlos Williams, from *Collected Poems 1939–1962, Volume II,* copyright © 1962 by William Carlos Williams. Reprinted by permission of New Directions Publishing Corp.

"The Cave" by David Brendan Hopes is used by permission of the author.

"A Christmas Hymn" from *Advice to a Prophet and Other Poems,* copyright © 1961 and renewed 1989 by Richard Wilbur. Reprinted by permission of Harcourt, Inc.

Cover design: Brad Norr Design
Cover art: *Fertile Crescent #2* by David Frey Utiger
Interior design: Wendy Holdman

This book was printed in the United States of America on acid-free paper.

Cowley Publications
4 Brattle Street • Cambridge, Massachusetts 02138
800-225-1534 • www.cowley.org

for Audrey Johnson
in memory of Ron Johnson

A stable-lamp is lighted
Whose glow shall wake the sky;
The stars shall bend their voices,
And every stone shall cry.
And every stone shall cry,
And straw like gold shall shine;
A barn shall harbor heaven,
A stall become a shrine.

FROM "A CHRISTMAS HYMN"
BY RICHARD WILBUR (B. 1921)

CONTENTS

Many have gone, and think me half a fool
To miss a day away in the cool country.
Maybe. But in a book I read and cherish,
Going to Walden is not so easy a thing
As a green visit. It is the slow and difficult
Trick of living, and finding it where you are.

MARY OLIVER, "GOING TO WALDEN"

⇛ PREFACE

$\mathcal{A}$s a college senior I read Henry David Thoreau's *Walden* for the first time. Once a week throughout the spring semester I discussed it in an independent study course with a professor of American History. We explored *Walden* and other works by Thoreau's contemporaries—Emerson, Walcott, Whitman—tracing streams and seepages of American Transcendentalism in thought, art, and architecture. As a young man from a farming town in southern Minnesota, and nearly ready to step out from my second "village home" of a small liberal arts college for a wider world, Thoreau's observations on vocation and life—his panning and sifting on the shore of Walden Pond for fresh American values—challenged my assumptions about the land and nature, about principled living and thoughtful residence in a place.

Thoreau's smooth prose surveyed every part of Walden Pond. His observations seemed to levitate over the woods around Concord, Massachusetts. He saw everything. He saw *through* things, and wrote *Walden* with consistent transparency. The book remains today clear as the water of Walden

Pond he knew then. Dip into it on almost any page and find
an example of Thoreau's lucid perception:

> Most men, even in this comparatively free country,
> through mere ignorance and mistake, are so occupied
> with the factitious cares and superfluously coarse
> labors of life that its finer fruits cannot be plucked by
> them. . . .

> That man who does not believe that each day contains
> an earlier, more sacred, and auroral hour than he has
> yet profaned, has despaired of life, and is pursuing a
> descending and darkening way. . . .

> I have lived some thirty years on this planet, and I
> have yet to hear the first syllable of valuable or even
> earnest advice from my seniors.

> It is the luxurious and the dissipated who set the fash-
> ions which the herd so diligently follow.

Most of the teachings I had received on spiritual matters
and ethical principles in my Lutheran church and home were
intended to order and arrange thought and action. These in-
structions provided a good, safe dwelling of life and belief, for
which I will always be grateful. Thoreau showed another way:
through parables and mesmerizing narration, he recorded a
freer kind of exploration. He seemed naturally at home in the
world, fearless and magnanimous. His world was boundless.
He was more like some kind of wild animal, unafraid of the
dark and at home in the woods, than like an author in a study.

I remember thinking as well that Thoreau's life was not far removed from the life of a hobo or a town clown. Certainly his fellow citizens, at home nearby in more conventional neighborhoods, thought that this philosopher and free-spirit was indeed an odd man. So close to the conventional neighborhoods of Concord, he found the shore of Walden Pond a world far removed from his neighbors' straight-line lives.

On one hand Thoreau's reasoned independence of purpose and his fierce, principled criticism of cultural norms, his humane regard for people and his naturalist's attention to the world seemed to flow from a well of knowledge and experience deep in soil far away from my own sources of life. On the other hand his thoughts had a strange, familiar appeal to me. I was aware that Thoreau wrote at the dawn of a new day in America. The country was waking to the promise and the threat of the Industrial Revolution. In the following decades other revolutions in technology and communication would transform America in ways unimagined by him. Still, Thoreau's nineteenth-century words ran freely and smoothly before my eyes, and I absorbed his clear ideas and compelling analysis with pleasure.

I write these words one hundred fifty years after the publication of *Walden* and twenty years after I first read it. I am seated in my church's study, at a desk facing east, in front of a large window. Outside is a grassy play area and beyond that many acres of suburban conservation land threaded with hiking trails. To the north two miles lies Walden Pond. Hundreds of times over the last decade, driving on Route 126, I have leaned into the wide curve of Concord Road as it rounds the pond. In warm weather I have stopped for swimmers and tourists on the crosswalk between the water and the parking lot. The duties and errands of my life—visits to hospitalized members of my parish, attendance at my boys' soccer games, oil changes at the car dealership on Route 2, appointments with my dentist in Lexington—pass Walden Pond, the lake which Thoreau wrote was "so remarkable for its depth and purity . . . a clear and deep green well, half a mile long and a mile and three quarters in circumference."

He thought that a lake such as Walden was "the landscape's most beautiful and expressive feature. It is earth's eye; looking into which the beholder measures the depth of his own nature." In admiration of Thoreau this book is about the way we see and perceive other familiar places of our lives.

As Thoreau settled into his little cabin just above Walden Pond, the horizons of his life expanded. As he became at home in his odd and particular location in the world, his perceptions of other places changed. He wrote of his time at Walden: "Both place and time were changed, and I dwelt nearer to those parts of the universe and to those eras in history which had most attracted me." This line from Thoreau will launch our discussions of the places we love.

For Thoreau, one small dwelling above the shore of a small body of water west of Boston could be the plot on which the imagination could set down roots and send forth blossoms and fruit. In this home place where Thoreau's determined imagination was nourished and exercised, all other worlds and panoramas, all other gardens and fields, all other hearths and homes, streamed in.

Throughout the book the reader will notice an interplay of thing and thought, of substance and imagination. In dialectics such as these, people have known and described the places they love. Poets and artists as well as scientists and scholars help us here. As they look at a thing-in-question from a different angle—bending the light in which it is seen, brightening and distorting the elements of it, and so on—they help the rest of us see the thing in new ways. Language works powerfully in comparing seemingly unlike things by rearranging words and meaning to let the familiarity of one thing lend insight into another, less familiar, thing or idea. In the Christian tradition these dialectics are sometimes conceived of as interplays of word and sacrament, of breath and clay, of the word heard and the word incarnate, of law and gospel.

The places we love go with us through our lives. Immigrants, travelers, foreigners and refugees, some longing to go home, some hoping to move on to a new home, carry a memory or a new vision of a beloved place in their minds. Following Thoreau, who sat beside his small hut near the shore of Walden Pond, this book invites the reader to "sit beside" the Bethlehem manger—a "place" many of us love—and there reflect on the other beloved places of our lives. The story of the nativity—known in the Bible in spare detail—may be an overlay for contemplation of other places we love.

This book is dedicated to my mother and to the memory of my father, her husband of fifty years. My mother still lives in the house on the edge of the Minnesota prairie in which my three brothers and I grew up. In that house our parents imagined a good home for us. That beloved place, along with some of the other places they loved, still shine for my wife, our two sons and me, in the constellation of locations by which we navigate together through each year.

Wayland, Massachusetts

HARBORS OF HEAVEN

Many are concerned about the monuments of the West and the East,—to know who built them. For my part, I should like to know who in those days did not build them,—who were above such trifling.

HENRY DAVID THOREAU (1817–1862), WALDEN

So we move from one to the other: from the shade under the baobab to the magic circle under heaven; from home to the public square, from suburb to city; from a seaside holiday to the enjoyment of the sophisticated arts, seeking for a point of equilibrium that is not of this world.

YI-FU TUAN (B. 1930), TOPOPHILIA

There are places I remember
all my life, though some have changed.
Some forever, not for better,
some have gone and some remain.

PAUL MCCARTNEY (B. 1942) AND
JOHN LENNON (1940–1980), "IN MY LIFE"

A PLACE OF ONE'S OWN

$\mathcal{A}$CCORDING TO THE SECOND CHAPTER of Luke's Gospel, when the Roman Emperor Augustus called for a "registration," citizens of his realm went to their hometowns to be counted and to pay a tax. Joseph went to Bethlehem, his ancestors' town. Scholars remind us that this census was a means of accumulating revenue and a method of controlling the population. The effect of this story is, for many Christians, benign. Hearing it told, they might be drawn to holiday thoughts. In the frenzy of commercial excess that marks the days before Christmas in America, this story has been known to calm and quiet frantic Christian consumers. This book invites readers to go to the Bethlehem of their imaginations. There will be no tax to pay, only the chance of a pleasant payoff, a windfall of enjoyment and appreciation of some of the places we love. The familiar and beloved images of the nativity will trigger thoughts of other birthplaces, hometowns, retreat houses, and final destinations.

Topophilia—Love of Place

Over thirty years ago, geographer Yi-Fu Tuan published a book titled *Topophilia*. This Greek word means "love of place." Professor Tuan's comparative study and analysis examines the human love of places from personal and cultural perspectives, showing how gender, age, ancestry, experience, education, and many other factors influence strong human attachments to certain places. Through the perception of the senses, learned cultural attitudes, systems of value and of ultimate meaning, human beings develop strong feelings for certain places on earth. Professor Tuan wrote that topophilia is, "as a concept, diffuse," but "as a personal experience, concrete and vivid."[1] In other words, a person might feel a strong sense of belonging in a place, a region, a large city, a small town, a neighborhood, a park, or an alley, without being able to say exactly why. The reasons for these attachments by human beings who seem to possess the technologies that enable them to live *anywhere* on earth but who choose to live in, remember, and long for *certain specific places*, are complex. Professor Tuan wrote:

> Topophilia takes many forms and varies greatly in emo-
> tional range and intensity. It is a start to describe what
> they are: fleeting visual pleasure; the sensual delight
> of physical contact; the fondness for place because it
> is familiar, because it is home and incarnates the past,
> because it evokes pride of ownership or of creation; joy
> in things because of animal health and vitality.[2]

The scope of my book is a dim reflection and a limited imitation of the ambition and range of Professor Tuan's scholarly

work. Two principles, not explicit or even present in his book, underlie my exploration of our human love of place.

1. The frame of this discussion is a Christian story.
This book is organized according to a story line from the Bible. The arguments follow a spiritual map known and imagined even by those in possession of the sparest knowledge of other biblical stories: the birth of Jesus recorded primarily in the Gospels of Matthew and Luke. The overlying trope of this study is that places we love may be "read" under and through the interpretive transparency of the story of Jesus' birth. To put the starting point succinctly: *Bethlehem, as a real and a legendary location, will stand as a symbol of other places we love.*

In the chapters that follow, Bethlehem, the birthplace of Jesus according to Christian tradition, will be a lens for thinking about *our* own places of origin: the villages and hamlets of our birth, the assemblages of family and friends attending our birthplaces in large urban medical centers, etc. The historical-critical question known to biblical scholars—should we call Bethlehem or Nazareth Jesus' hometown?—reflects a biographical ambiguity known to many contemporary Americans. Born in city hospitals, during their childhoods they moved several times with their families. With no village full of extended families and stories to call home, they are likely to be among a vast mass of citizens orbiting urban centers, pursuing their lives in suburban schools, office cubicles, and shopping malls.

In the month of December, many people place nativity scenes on mantels, under Christmas trees, in church sanctuaries, and on front lawns. The centerpiece of each of these installations—these Bethlehems of our imagination—is a manger containing a figure of the infant Jesus. The other characters from the biblical nativity stories stand, sit, or kneel around the manger. This grouping is placed within a miniature stable. Later we will ponder the significance and meaning of this structure.

Joseph, the attending father, will stand for the parent who helps define a beloved place on earth. The small town or village as an idealized place of origin and refuge will be contemplated in the inspiration of Joseph's ancestral hometown of Bethlehem. He and Mary, the mother of Jesus, represent to Christians the ideal of loving parents. For very young children, the parents' presence is all that is needed to make a place beloved. In fact the mother *is* the world for the newborn child. The voice of the mother, the face and touch of the mother, are the movable and only essential features of the young child's beloved place.

Finally, the holy city of Jerusalem, north of Bethlehem, casts shade in the day and light at night over every little town of our imaginations. The great city of God, as city and symbol, supports outlying villages economically, politically, and spiritually; it supports our wandering lives—especially in a sacramental imagination—as our common destination, a city that will receive us all. In the biography of Jesus, Jerusalem was the destination of the holy family for the dedication of the baby in the temple. The holy city was his adult destination as well. The events of his final days in Jerusalem overlaid new meaning on the city's sacred history. Jerusalem remains for us today an important symbol of struggle and of peace for great numbers of people of several faiths. This eye-of-the-hurricane city is still the eschatological city of hope and the capital of the kingdom of God.

2. The work of some literary artists, mainly poets, illuminates the images, themes, and spiritual cartography outlined above.

Wallace Stevens, William Carlos Williams, Vassar Miller, Richard Wilbur, and Frank Conroy will be the chief guides in our exploration. Poets, along with artists and children, are among those human beings who have been known to sit in corners of rooms, at the crossroads of wooded paths, on the tops of hills and at the outskirts of cities, in search of words to reflect the fullness of their situation and their placement in the world. A beloved place may be a familiar corner of a garden, an imaginary cottage in the woods, the favorite corner of our childhood yard, a community's utopian dreamland, a farmer's field, an alley in a city, the setting of a novel.

The French philosopher Gaston Bachelard, in his study of "felicitous space," wrote that "If a poet looks through a microscope or a telescope, he always sees the same thing."[3] As a child might enjoy the focusing lens of a camera, zooming in and out for different perspectives of the same thing, this book zooms in and out on some of the primary focal points of the Bethlehem nativity as a symbol and archetype of the places we love.

Imagining a Place

One's place may be the spot where one feels one *belongs,* or it may be the location in which one's imagination is at home. The perception of belonging is useful for the purposes of this book. The place one loves may not be the place one happens to occupy at a given moment. The place one loves more likely might be the place in which one *has been,* and then recalls, or it might be the faraway place to which one *hopes to go.* Our sense of place—our love of place—draws in large measure on memories and on dreams for the future, and on the coalescence of memories and dreams. Some people live in a pleasant tension between the memory of the places to which they have been and places to which they hope to go. The chapters of this book examine the places we love as birthplace, family place, house and home, hometown, and finally the destined and comprehensive community of the city of God. The multifaceted tropes for this analysis are the birth narratives of Jesus in the Gospels of Matthew and Luke.

These brief biblical narratives have been interrogated and qualified as history, myth, tradition, religious propaganda, etc., but behind the archaeological, anthropological, theological, literary, religious, and other types of analysis of and commentary on the infancy narratives, lies a simple story. The imagination grasps it immediately. This book is about the stories of each of our lives told in terms of places. In each of these places our imaginations have been engaged and have formed a beloved place out of a space that our bodies and our possessions occupy. A brief theological excursion will set the stage.

The Earth as God's Beloved Place

Places we love are those to which we return, if only in our memories, as we recreate and re-imagine them. We return to these places *because* we love them. In some sense the place we love *possesses us.* The act of imagining often is motivated by love. Parents might imagine a home for their children. Out of love for one another and for their children they possess the power *to provide* at least an approximation of that home. In his tree-house fort a child imagines for himself the site of thrilling imaginary adventures. The primal narrative of this kind of love-at-work, imagining a world into being, is recorded in the first chapters of Genesis:

> In the beginning when God created the heavens and the earth, the earth was a formless void and darkness covered the face of the deep, while a wind from God swept over the face of the waters. Then God said, "Let there be light."
>
> (GENESIS 1:1–3)

The world is recited into being. Out of the imagination of God, creation becomes an event and the world becomes the stage. The ancient author of this part of Genesis uses dialectical tropes of light and darkness, of water and dry land, composed in "stanzas" or rounds of evening and morning, one day following another. *The world* is the place God has imagined and formed through the creative power of "words spoken." The world is the place God loves.

The first stanza of W. H. Auden's poem "Words" reads:

> A sentence uttered makes a world appear
> Where all things happen as it says they do;
> We doubt the speaker, not the tongue we hear:
> Words have no word for words that are not true.[4]

The word is the powerful, creating force in the world. As it is *said,* so it *shall be.* A beloved place is so because we *say* it is, or someone we trust says that it is, and so we believe it.

The final stanza of the creation narrative in Genesis 1 imagines a resting place. The sabbath is a spiritual "place" organically connected to the work of reciting a beloved world into being.

Thus the heavens and the earth were finished, and all their multitude. And on the seventh day God finished the work that he had done, and he rested on the seventh day from all the work that he had done.

(GENESIS 2:1–2)

The world is the place-in-space called into being by God's creative imagination.

A Holy Place

Scholars of the history and theology of biblical languages tell us that the uses of Hebrew and Greek words translated into English as forms of the word *holy* bear several related meanings, some of them central to the theology of Jews and Christians. To say that God is holy is to say that God is wholly other than we. God is pure and complete in being, mysterious and awesome, etc. Holy places, holy things, holy words, holy people acquire the quality of holiness by identification with or participation in God's word and therefore in God's will and therefore in God's holiness. In the Bible there are cultic and communal, ethical and legal, ritual and spiritual aspects of holiness. For the purpose of this book, a pre-prophetic biblical lineage of the concept of holiness helps. In this theology of holiness, and the Lord's holy resting places—the top of Mt. Sinai, the sanctuary of the tent of meeting,[5] and the Temple at Jerusalem for example—are the places in which smoke and fire are the signs of the divine presence. In imitation of God the Creator, human beings make places for themselves in the world. As the places we love are the *products* of our creative imaginations, they are also "living" partners with us in our days on earth. The places we love may have power over every part of our being. The places we love "speak" to us, rejuvenate us, and offer us rest. The seventh day in Genesis is the spiritual end-stop of the poem of creation. The sabbath is a silent place-in-time. The poetry of creation that called the world into being is ended, and a restful silence follows, but even in the sabbath time-out-of-time, the creation speaks its "words."

John of Patmos

The poet and visionary John of Patmos, who imagined the world of God's apocalypse, wrote words that have comforted and encouraged multitudes with the imagining of a place that would one day dominate the scape of life:

> I saw the holy city, the new Jerusalem, coming down out of heaven from God, prepared as a bride adorned for her husband. And I heard a loud voice from the throne saying, "See, the home of God is among mortals."
>
> (REVELATION 21:2–3)

The solitary literary artist may create a world of imagination that imitates the world of salvation presented in the scriptures.

The key of entry into the poet's world might be a certain sensitivity to aesthetic qualities of thought and language. The key of entry into the vision of scripture might be faith. When one has "entered" either the world of the poet or the world of Revelation's apocalyptic vision, one will have arrived at a certain created "place." If this is not a place of pleasure and enjoyment, it may be a place of importance and meaning, even of ultimate meaning.

Jewish and Christian scripture laid before sympathetic readers and listeners a world that participates in timelines and history, customs of everyday life, politics, war, and so on, but the biblical world is not identical with those aspects of life. The words of the Bible create and constitute a world *apart,* an inspired and altogether different world into which people may "place" themselves as residents, wanderers, or observers. In the public reading of scripture, worshipers listen as if the ancient words were about their own lives and times. By imaginatively locating themselves within the world of scripture, a Sunday-morning listener inherits a sacred "place." This is the nature of the scripture's holiness: The world it constitutes may be a sanctuary, a retreat, a holy homeland arrived at through the imagination in a plane of existence parallel with a person's everyday life.

Every place that a person loves is overlaid with meaning. Memory, imagination, determined purpose all contribute to the creation of a beloved place out of a mere setting or location. In summary, *the imagination creates a place.* The creative imagination might be motivated by love. A first principle of Christian theology is that love is a powerful force, not a passive regard. Love creates worlds, changes outlooks, alters plans, renews expectations, etc. Love may create a place, and other people in turn may respond to that place in strong and lasting ways. A powerful, sustained vision from a single literary artist or, as in the case of the Jewish and Christian scriptures, the products of the connected, corporate imaginations of generations of authors—each one in possession of a piece of a vision of the kingdom of God—create a "place" in which others feel at home.

Bethlehem

The chapters that follow explore and ponder the Bethlehem of our corporate and private imaginations. We will begin by bending down to the manger in the center of the stable. In many imaginative interpretations, the manger is a small wooden trough for the feeding of animals. Whatever the Bethlehem manger "was"—an indentation in the rock of a cave, a soft bed of sand—is of little importance. In the Christian imagination the manger and the encircling stable are the centerpiece of our imagination, around which the whole world stirs from sleep and snaps to attention. The Bethlehem manger defines the center of the place we love. Its location in our imaginations establishes the center of an extraordinary "place" to which we might return in seasonal remembrance, worship, and devotion. In a similar way a literary artist might create through her work worlds that readers might enter. These extraordinary worlds overlay and participate in the features of the ordinary world of human experience but are not identical with the ordinary. One such artist was the poet Wallace Stevens. Chapter One considers his vision and artistic creations.

Give me my scallop shell of quiet,
My staff of faith to walk upon . . .

SIR WALTER RALEIGH (1552–1618),
"THE PASSIONATE MAN'S PILGRIMAGE"

. . . this study is devoted to insignificant things. Occasionally they reveal strange subtleties. In order to bring them out I shall place them under the magnifying glass of the imagination.

GASTON BACHELARD (1884–1962),
THE POETICS OF SPACE

In life, no house, no home
My Lord on earth might have;
In death, no friendly tomb
But what a stranger gave.
What may I say? Heaven was his home;
But mine the tomb wherein he lay.

SAMUEL CROSSMAN (1624–1683)

One

THE MANGER

NEWBORN BABIES, partially hidden under a quilt or in their mother's arms, attract the attention of adults. Gaston Bachelard wrote,

> [W]henever life seeks to shelter, protect, cover or hide itself, the imagination sympathizes with the being that inhabits the protected space. The imagination experiences protection in all its nuances of security, from life in the most material of shells, to more subtle concealment through imitation of surfaces.[1]

The manger which in our imaginations contained and held the infant Jesus is the center of this book. The manger defines all territory around it. The stable, village, fields, roads, and distant cities in our nativity scenes—and in our minds' eyes, at the rereading and retelling of the Christmas story—are given definition and fame by the manger that holds the baby.

Christians might say that the ungilded manger-for-a-crib establishes the whole world around it as a beloved place. The Christian teaching of the incarnation means that the earth is good, blessed and visited by God.

A beloved place might be said to be a "container" of life. When we are comfortable and at home in a place—as an infant sleeps comfortably in a crib, then later in life feels at home in a certain room, in a neighborhood, a park, in a region of the country, and so on—our satisfaction and comfort may be said to come from a sense of being "held" by the particular shape of the place we love. Small containers of life will be the first objects considered in this chapter, with the Bethlehem manger of Luke's Gospel as the chief and primary example. Other types, images, and symbols of life-contained—the shell and the tomb—will be noted briefly. The cave as a container of life will help us move our thoughts outward to the stable; then our attention will move outward to the shelters of our imagination that stand over the manger. The twentieth-century poet Wallace Stevens will be this chapter's keynote literary artist. We will examine two of his poems: "Anecdote of a Jar" and "A Rabbit as King of the Ghosts."

Held in Place: Wallace Stevens

Aristotle (384–322 BC) defined a human sense of "place" in terms of a container. He wrote in his *Physics* that "place is thought to be a kind of surface, and as it were, a vessel, i.e., a container of the thing." In other words, a thing or a person is "held" in place. This fragment of a philosophical thought will be the beginning of our discussion of the Bethlehem manger, the centerpiece of a place loved and occupied by many people through their imaginations and their faith.

The placement of the manger in Bethlehem creates an accessible scene to which the mind and the emotions may attend. If one is not too literal-minded about it, one might say that the Bethlehem manger was "placed" in Bethlehem by God to recreate the world and to center it there in an outdoor shelter, open to the elements and to the transporting currents of the spirit and accessible to human imaginations. The placing of the birth-manger in Bethlehem created a common homestead of the heart, located in the text of a story cherished by communities and congregations.

Wallace Stevens (1875–1955) was a Hartford, Connecticut insurance executive and an accomplished modernist poet. No friend of conventional religion, he claimed that he threw out his Bible with the kitchen trash and was happy to have the whole pile out the house. He tried to create poems out of the pure perception of his imagination, without the constraints of history or tradition.

Stevens wrote poems full of bright, exotic sounds, curious images, and unusual views of the world. Commenting on a volume of Stevens's poems, Robert Lowell wrote, "[Stevens's] places are places visited on a vacation."[2] By this, Lowell must not have meant that Stevens's places were like travel-guide descriptions or historical overviews for tourists. They are rather more like reflections of the way a person might *feel* about a place visited on vacation. Without work or home responsibilities and without regular social connections, a person in a vacation destination occupies a place where the imagination can run free. A certain lightness or levity characterizes the mood and outlook of one released from everyday concerns. In Stevens's poems there are places lit by "the obscure moon lighting an obscure world" and colored by "the ruddy temper, the hammer / Of red and blue." To put Lowell's comment in the language of religion, one might say that Wallace Stevens's places are those one might visit in a sabbath state of mind, in a moment of rest when the imagination is set free to find its own scenic views and campgrounds on which to set up temporary shelters.

Stevens's poems strike some thoughtful readers as impenetrable. This might be due in part to our reading habit of looking for historical references, biographical reasons, cultural commentary, and other kinds of explanatory material behind an immediately puzzling poem. The abstract nature of a poem may disconcert readers, but abstraction may also broaden and strengthen their range of perceptions about the world.

In an address at Harvard University in 1945 Stevens said, "[W]e live in the description of a place and not in the place itself."[3] He imagined and created his own world through his poems. Readers who respond to a poet-of-the-imagination such as Stevens are able to enter the poet's world and to discover there places momentarily "habitable" through their imaginations. Creating his poetic universe by the union of the reality most of us have in common and his personal imagination, Stevens called his creation the *supreme fiction.* Frank Kermode wrote of Stevens's body of work, "Over the skeleton of reality the mind weaves its always changing, always delightful, fictive covering. . . . This is not a rational world."[4]

Stevens's poem "Anecdote of a Jar" interprets the imagination's creation of a place out of an undifferentiated space. The first two stanzas read:

> I placed a jar in Tennessee,
> And round it was, upon a hill.
> It made the slovenly wilderness
> Surround that hill.

The wilderness rose up to it,
And sprawled around, no longer wild.
The jar was round upon the ground
And tall and of a port in air.[5]

In the fictive[6] reality of the poem, setting a jar on a wooded hill in Tennessee makes the location around it different (or so it seems) from the rest of the wilderness, and the reader of the poem imagines the defining of a place: a jar gives and is given geographical location and a place.

There is a purity of placement in the strange and lyrical line "I placed a jar in Tennessee." Reading it one might be amused as the proportions of things—of surveying lots, specifying locations, finding one's way, the shape of a mason jar, its proper use and disposal, etc.—are called into question and pondered. "Anecdote of a Jar" is not exactly a poem *about* creation; it is more like a poem *of* creation. Thinking about the poem, a reader's thoughts might be drawn to the creation of art and to the imaginative creation of a distinctive or beloved place apart from all other places. Even though complex and sophisticated thought might have gone into the writing of the poem, Stevens did not write it to fit a reader's assumptions of a rational order of argument or as a reasonable, progressive description or instruction.

The world of Stevens's poems, and of this poem in particular, is not a rational world, to be sure. However, as a helium-filled balloon must be tied to some earthbound anchor so that it doesn't sail through the air and out of sight, the enjoyment of its color, buoyancy, and texture lost to human senses on the ground, a vision—poetic or religious—must be anchored to the features of the world we all know in ordinary conversation, newspaper articles, history books, and maps. Stevens's poetic vision is tied and tacked to ordinary experience—sounds, sights, emotions, and places we all know—even as the arrangement of these things and their relationships are adjusted in the art. The nativity story defines a place in our imaginations, but it is tied down, in Luke's Gospel for example, in specific ways: "In those days a decree went out from Emperor Augustus that all the world should be registered. This was the first registration and was taken while Quirinius was governor of Syria" (2:1–2). In a similar way, if Stevens's created order of things is not a *rational* world, it is a *particular* world. As "I placed a jar in Tennessee" seems to specify a certain few inches of ground on the surface of the earth, Stevens's poems are filled with references to other actual places on American soil. Kermode wrote,

> We ought to remind ourselves, if the need arises, of the prevalence of American usage and place-names in Stevens' poems, and of his insistence that reality is what you see finely and imagine fully from where you are and as what you are; as, for example, on an ordinary evening in New Haven.[7]

In summary, two points related to our topic of beloved places and to the Bethlehem manger may be drawn from Wallace Stevens's poem. One is a particular point about the container/jar/manger. The other is a general point, drawn from Stevens's approach to poetry, about the imagination and creation of places.

First, "Anecdote of a Jar" is like a simple, dispassionate laboratory examination of the creative act of defining a place. In

Stevens's poem, the jar contains nothing, but it could contain many things. Unexpectedly, the empty jar "holds" the world around it in place. The Bethlehem manger contains Jesus as a peasant infant, without words or proper shelter. Gospel readers know that this infant lying there in that crude container has held Christian readers in wonder and faith. A spiritual song enjoyed by generations of children repeats that he *holds the whole world in his hands.* The one *held* there, in that makeshift crib of a manger, holds our attention. In Christian theology, and in the conviction of a faithful person, Jesus holds the world. In Luke's words, Jesus, born in Bethlehem, is the one appointed and sent by God the Father. He is the creative and authoritative Lord of all.

The empty jar that gives shape to the wilderness around it might cause some Christians to think not only of the Bethlehem manger but also—and perhaps more vividly—of the Jerusalem tomb of Jesus. Every day, Christian pilgrims from all over the world visit the Church of the Holy Sepulcher in the Old City of Jerusalem. They mill around outside the church and line up inside the church's rotunda, a room cared for by Greek Orthodox and Armenian clergy but "owned" by Christians everywhere. They enter a small chamber in the middle of the rotunda. Inside this chamber they see nothing. This empty space, as medieval maps showed, is the center of the world. As Stevens's empty jar gives definition to the wilderness in Tennessee, the empty tomb redefines the spiritual geography of the world around it.

Second, a point that has been made and will be repeated in the chapters that follow: the imagination is the power of creation. The implications of this statement apply to a number of endeavors and fields of life, including business, religious piety, and ethics, as well as art: The world is what one imagines, what one envisions, what one conceives and is able to communicate to others through a business plan, a doctrine of faith, a pattern of right action or, as in the case of Stevens, a poem. The suggestive, reality-shaping power of the imagination can claim, define, and name our world as well as the world of our ancestors and the world to come. Stepping out into the Roman Empire and claiming it as the kingdom of God (cf. Luke 4:43), Jesus envisioned for his followers a new reality, local places and the widest expanses of space and time, as God's world. Inhabiting this world would be people whose minds and imaginations could be cleansed and inspired by the original imaginative Spirit that created the world. Old words from the prophet Joel, quoted by the writer of Luke's Gospel, would have new meaning:

> In the last days it will be, God declares,
> that I will pour out my Spirit upon all flesh,
> and your sons and your
> daughters shall prophesy,
> and your young men shall see visions,
> and your old men shall dream dreams.
>
> (ACTS 2:17)

The imagination creates a beloved place.

Another self-consciously American writer thought, as Wallace Stevens did, that heaven and earth are brought together in the imagination. Henry David Thoreau might not have conceived of his own creative work as a *mundo* the way Stevens did. He might not have thought that he was the creator of a universe, but Thoreau believed and imagined that the whole world was available to him in the woods around Walden Pond. As a writer and philosopher, Thoreau could see and know the general shape of life on earth on the shore of a small lake northwest of Boston.

The Metaphor of Place: Henry David Thoreau

Wallace Stevens and Henry David Thoreau, two New Englanders separated by about a hundred years in time, were worlds apart with regard to their personal lifestyles. Both writers, however, knew the poetic nature of place. The theologian Ray Hart, commenting that Stevens was a direct literary descendant of Thoreau, wrote that each one might have agreed that

> things have their place in metaphor . . . placement is incorrigibly metaphorical. If there are no springs of natural poetry at the headwaters of human sensibility, nature withers under a most unnatural sun.[8]

Things are in place, and thereby have meaning, in metaphor. Metaphor is the transportation vehicle of language. As planes, trains, and cars carry people from place to place, make connections, accommodate commerce, service, and all other actions and interactions of human survival and society, metaphors carry meaning from here to there, making connections, coloring the world with order and sense. When metaphors are at work creating new meaning, a house becomes a home, a geographic outcrop becomes a sacred mountain, an astronomical phenomenon becomes an emotional event.

Wallace Stevens called the created world of his poetry his *mundo* to distinguish it from the world of concrete facts, but, as mentioned above, his *mundo* is full of actual experiences, observations, real events, and objects—like evenings in New Haven, the changing appearances of the sea, and the sound of birdcalls. Out of this material of the natural world, Stevens recreated a new world of sense, perception, and facts in his poems. Similarly, Thoreau's deep "seeing" of Walden as situated between earth and the heavens—and participating in the color of both—seems similar to Stevens's noting the power of "fictive imagination" that brings heaven to earth.[9] Stevens and Thoreau saw and wrote about worlds in unusual ways. Each had a particular creative genius for seeing the world in extraordinary lights and shades of light. The products of their imaginations—their poems and essays—have changed the way their readers see their own worlds.

The human imagination is a powerful creative faculty. We might even say that who we are depends on what we imagine ourselves to be. The Christian faith is in large part a matter of finding and applying images to one's life and to the world. In the examination of our lives and, through faith, the application of Christian images to our lives, we might make adjustments to our self-images. The gospel of Jesus Christ invites people to see themselves as God's children and as citizens of a great and beloved place, the kingdom of God. Through confession, forgiveness of sins, study of scripture, and the application of images of faith, people may re-imagine new identities and new purposes for themselves, so that the world might appear in a new light. Through the power of the imagination the world will have been recreated in accord with the song of an ancient poet who imagined the world as a beloved place:

The earth is the LORD's and all that is in it,
  the world, and those who live in it;
for he has founded it on the seas,
  and established it on the rivers.

(PSALM 24:1–2)

The psalmist imagined himself as a person alive in the presence of God. The product of God's imagination was all around him. In this song he confessed God's power and authority, centered in the temple, the holy and beloved place and the capital of God's reign. Even if our imaginations are not drenched in God's word, as the psalmist's was, we all imagine ourselves in some relation to objects and to other forces and aspects of the world, such as seasons, weather, and landscapes. One more poem by Wallace Stevens will be useful in our discussion.

While Psalm 24 is a good example of how a God-fearing, thankful human being, immersed in the faith of his or her ancestors, imagines the world around him, Stevens's poem "A Rabbit as King of the Ghosts" is a metaphor of self-consciousness and of being "in place" from the fictive point of view of a rabbit. The poem is an example of what it might feel like for a rabbit—or in different circumstances, for a person—to be comfortably in place.

To be, in the grass, in the peacefullest time,
Without that monument of cat,
The cat forgotten in the moon;

And to feel that the light is a rabbit-light,
In which everything is meant for you
And nothing need be explained;

Then there is nothing to think of. It comes of itself;
And east rushes west and west rushes down,
No matter. The grass is full

And full of yourself. The trees around are for you,
The whole of the wideness of night is for you, A self
that touches all edges.[10]

Luke writes that the angels knew that a baby lying in a manger would mean a lot to the shepherds:

> In that region there were shepherds living in the fields,
> keeping watch over their flock by night. Then an angel
> of the Lord stood before them, and the glory of the
> Lord shone around them, and they were terrified. But
> the angel said to them, "Do not be afraid; for see—I am
> bringing you good news of great joy for all the people:
> to you is born this day in the city of David a Savior,
> who is the Messiah, the Lord. This will be a sign for
> you: you will find a child wrapped in bands of cloth
> and lying in a manger."
>
> (LUKE 2:8–12)

The first seven verses of Luke 2 carry the reader's attention
downward from the great and powerful name of Caesar to
the newborn baby lying close to the ground. The verses chan-
nel the reader inward from an expansive world empire to a
small implement of rural life somewhere in the vicinity of
Bethlehem. Luke begins with the Roman Emperor's royal decree and within a few lines draws our eyes to a baby, born and

held in a serviceable but less than desirable manner in the animals' feed trough. The literary dynamic in these verses is an emotional compression and explosion. The reader's thoughts are pressed down from the great to the small where an irony erupts: this small one in the animals' trough is greater than the Roman Emperor.

The next verse is a moment of spatial relaxation as the narrative retreats to an unspecified field in a region outside town. The telescoping "lens" of the passage moves the reader in and out from the Judean hills under the night sky to that shelter of animals on the edge of town, from the broad, heavenly vision of angels in the air to the picture of an infant in a manger on the ground.

The Manger

In his book *The Liberation of Christmas,* the scholar Richard Horsley writes about the Bethlehem manger:

> That the child is laid in a feeding trough for animals literally and socially places the messiah and savior on a level with the lowly shepherds, in complete contrast with Caesar Augustus. . . . That the child is laid in a manger . . . is declared to be the sign for the shepherds that the savior, the messiah and lord, has been born in the city of David . . . a sign usually affects or is directly related to the people addressed in the message.[11]

The baby in a manger was a sign for simple shepherds. The manger-holding-a-baby also functions for us as a multifaceted centerpiece of our attention. We most often imagine the manger as a small crib—not much larger than a baby's body—cradling the child. Without the baby, the manger would still mark the center of the world to the animals that feed from it. As a container it could still define a place—maybe a placid farm scene or a rural tableau. As a cradle of Jesus, spiritually speaking, one might say that for many Christians it defines the axis of the world and the turning of the year.

Despised and unsheltered shepherds have not been alone in their immediate reaction to the announcement of a child lying in a manger. Children, who may identify with the shepherds' freedom from confinement and the supervision of adults, are drawn in fascination to the baby:

> Away in a manger, no crib for a bed,
> The little Lord Jesus lay down his sweet head.

Adult commentators have analyzed the manger crib as a foreshadow of Jesus' rejection by his own people. Children and others with a childlike outlook have seen the manger as a sign of radical accessibility and of boundless possibility. Around this baby in the manger is another place for children: a nursery, a playhouse.

Bible dictionaries and commentaries tell us that the Bethlehem manger of Luke 2 might have been a box or a container made of wood or carved out of rock. Western Christians most often imagine a manger of wood, but if we can imagine it made of other material, a connection may be drawn to other "cribs" of life—burrows, nests, and seashells, for example—and some general observations about this kind of life-container may be made.

In *The Poetics of Space*, Gaston Bachelard devotes a chapter to the image of the shell.[12] He writes about the human sense of wonder at soft, living things inhabiting the "rocks" of seashells, which are like hard nests of life, polished by the sea and the sand.

The Seashell

The seashell is an ancient symbol of Christian baptism. In the sacrament of rebirth—in which an old self is drowned and a new self rises with Christ—the shell is a multifaceted poetic image of life and death. A useful cup for dipping and pouring if used for the actual baptism, the shell, especially an intact bivalve, is an image of the tomb but also suggestive of a boat, a floating vessel of refuge on the sea. Together in assembly, the baptized sail through life, often seated in the church's nave, which is the ship of rescue (as in Noah's ark) sent to hold God's chosen people over the waves of life. The shell that holds the people of God safely through life may sail through other elements and states of consciousness. For example, Vassar Miller's poem "Lullaby for a Grown Man" begins:

> Laced in your shell of sleep,
> Lie here secure from sorrow
> And dread and need to weep
> Till hatched anew tomorrow.[13]

Luke's Gospel sets the tone for a night-time imagining of the birth of Jesus: "In that region there were shepherds living in the fields, keeping watch over their flock by night" (2:8). Places we love are often most vividly imagined set in a frame of darkness.

Asleep on the Hay

In a wide view, the night sky is the shell that holds life. People alive on earth have always found the dark sky, inset with stars, to be among the richest spiritual stages before their eyes. Sleep, as the individual's entry into the darkness of night, is the spiritual as well as the physical place of rest and renewal. Sleep is the darkness of the womb and of the tomb; it is the unconscious "other land" into which one "dies" and from which one may return, changed. Samuel Daniel, a poet who lived at the end of the sixteenth century, wrote:

> Care-charmer sleep, son of the sable night,
> Brother to death, in silent darkness born,
> Relieve my languish, and restore the light;
> With dark forgetting of my care, return.

If in the Christian imagination the Bethlehem manger is the shell of life from which the world is born again—on account of the one who lies in it—it is also a miniature image of the tomb, another rock of life from which life rises renewed.

The Tomb

If Christians can find a way to meditate on the meaning of the nativity apart from the overwhelming clang and jingle of the winter holiday, they will note how the story of the birth of Jesus foreshadows his death. In the Christian gospel theology, both the birth and the death are important "saving" events, and they share the same story line. The birth takes place outside the regular shelter of Bethlehem, the City of David. The death occurs outside the walls of David's capital city, Jerusalem. Mary, Jesus' mother, is of course present beside her newborn child, and she is beside him as he suffers and dies. With her at the birth are the local rabble, the startled shepherds from the fields around Bethlehem; at the death she is accompanied by the remnant of his followers and onlookers from the streets of Jerusalem.

"Christmas Mourning," a poem by Vassar Miller, interprets this birth-death connection in the life story of Jesus. The poem is constructed of a substance and in tone colors that might be immediately incomprehensible to those of us conditioned to think of Christmas as a commercial holiday in which the gospel characters are featured next to Santa Claus in a long-running juiced-up promotion. The poem begins:

> On Christmas Day I weep
> Good Friday to rejoice.
> I watch the Child asleep.
> Does He half dream the choice
> The Man must make and keep?
>
> At Christmastime I sigh
> For my Good Friday hope.
> Outflung the Child's arms lie
> To span in their brief scope
> The death the Man must die.[14]

This is a poem of wisdom and the product of a mature theological imagination as well as a model of a telescoping method of thinking about the places we love. Moving in and out from the center to the horizon, it sees the end at the beginning and is able to look forward in time and backward in memory in a single dynamic view.

Of course Vassar Miller was not the first to note the foreshadowing of Jesus' death in details of the narration of his birth. For example, myrrh, the third gift of the wise men according to Matthew (after gold and frankincense), was used to anoint the body in death. This child king, Jesus, would conquer death and reign over his people even in that enemy territory beyond the grave.[15] The poetic reverberations heard in the rhyming of the words *grave* and *cave* are a combination that unlocks the imagination's window on the theology of our topic.

British businessman William Dix (1837–1898) wrote the carol "What Child Is This?" The second verse reads:

Why lies he in such mean estate
Where ox and ass are feeding?
Good Christian, fear; for sinners here
The silent Word is pleading.

Nails, spear shall pierce him through,
The cross be borne for me, for you;
Hail, hail the Word made flesh,
The babe, the son of Mary!

These lyrics conform to the circle of life and death and so help us fully envision the beloved human place. The sheltering stable of the Bethlehem scene often is imagined as a cave. The tomb of Jesus in a garden outside of the walls of Jerusalem is most often imagined as a kind of cave as well. The cave—a hollow in the earth or in rock—suggests a place of shelter and the location of a birth. One would find arguments that the Bethlehem manger was actually sheltered in a cave or, as one Roman Catholic guide puts it, "in a grotto which would have been part of the house."[16] The second-level shelter, above the manger, is the subject of the next chapter.

The ox knows its owner,
    and the donkey its master's crib;
but Israel does not know,
    my people do not understand.

ISAIAH 1:3

"Home," he mocked gently.
"Yes, what else but home?
It all depends on what you mean by home."

ROBERT FROST (1874–1963),
"THE DEATH OF THE HIRED MAN"

Let us settle ourselves, and work and wedge our feet downward through the mud and slush of opinion, and prejudice, and tradition, and delusion, and appearance, that alluvion which covers the globe, through Paris and London, through New York and Boston and Concord, through Church and State, through poetry and philosophy and religion, til we come to a hard bottom and rocks in place, which we can call reality.

HENRY DAVID THOREAU (1817–1862), *WALDEN*

Two

THE STABLE

$\mathcal{L}$UKE 2:6–7, the two verses that sketch and frame the outline of the scene surrounding the Bethlehem manger, have been interpreted imaginatively for thousands of years. Some readers and commentators continue to shade the characters, and color the scene emotionally, with circumstances of inconvenience and hardship. They emphasize crowded conditions, callous disregard for the mother and her newborn son, and an inhospitable property owner. The same verses have been meditated on in a very different light and emotional color: as a comfortable nursery set up by caring adults, a warm night, a suitable if unconventional crib. This chapter moves outward from the manger and other small containers of life to shelters that surround and more broadly define the places we love. The model for our imaginations throughout this chapter is the stable, well known from December nativity scenes. In popular holiday props and depictions, the stable forms a roof over the manger. The stable is the frame of a house, and the house is a kind of human cradle. Bachelard wrote:

> Without [the house] man would be a dispersed being. It maintains him through the storms of the heavens and through those of life. It is body and soul. It is the human being's first world. Before he is "cast into the world," as claimed by certain hasty metaphysics, man is laid in the cradle of the house. And always, in our daydreams, the house is a large cradle.[1]

Standing between the canopy of the stable and the focal point of the manger are human figures, their bodies forming a shelter of attention and concern. The next chapter considers the *people* whose presence—standing by, encircling, congregating, gathering—make an extraordinary place out of an ordinary piece of ground. The sections of the present chapter study the Bethlehem stable of our imaginations—the frame of the most familiar icon of faith for Christians—under four images: the peasant hut; the spirit house; the sabbath house, offering rest and communion in conformance with Jewish and Christian traditions; and the cave, or the shelter of stone that carries perhaps its own historical accuracy and certainly its own theo-poetic power.

Sheltered by the Imagination

Richard Wilbur's "A Christmas Hymn" places the stable of our imaginations in traditional perspective.

> A stable lamp is lighted
> Whose glow shall wake the sky;

The stars shall bend their voices,
And every stone shall cry.
And every stone shall cry,
And straw like gold shall shine;
A barn shall harbor heaven,
A stall become a shrine.[2]

Wilbur was born in New York City in 1921 and today is one of America's most distinguished and honored poets. This poem was written in the late 1950s at the request of a colleague for a holiday program at Wesleyan University in Middletown, Connecticut. It paints a verbal picture of a stable that fits most conventional American images of the wood-framed nativity scene.

In the sixteenth century Albrecht Dürer illustrated his *Nativity* as a German farmhouse. A historian wrote of this image:

A farmstead is shown with many corners and nooks. . . . A locality of this kind would not have been found anywhere in Germany. The imagination wants to express its fancies here, as well as in the open landscape with its mountains.[3]

The image of the stable is so attractive and full of emotional and religious meaning that the human imagination finds many ways to fill in the sketchy outline of the birth story. A recent exhibition of nativity scenes from around the world showed cultural differences and developing social and theological meanings. For example, some current German nativities include an image of Santa Claus, and Central American scenes show the devil, turning his back from the central characters.

This notion will be mentioned again in relation to a William Carlos Williams poem in Chapter Three.

In addition to setting a traditional Northern European–American nativity scene, the theology of the poem is a good example of the telescoping perspective and poetic dynamic central to this book. For Richard Wilbur, as for Vassar Miller, an important piece of Christian thought lies behind this poetic perspective: the end of things is present—and may be foreseen by those who have eyes to see—in the beginning. In the Hebrew book of Isaiah and the New Testament book of Revelation, these two limits are located in one being and body: "I am the first and the last; besides me there is no other."[4] In a full theological imagining of the nativity, God's word is present and alive as the first word as well as the last word of life. At the beginning—and in any given middle moment of existence—the book of life is not yet read through or fully known, even as the author of the whole story is confessed as Lord.

The final stanza of Wilbur's Christmas poem ties together loose strands of human experience and meaning. In duration and extent the horizons of life have been drawn down to a particular point on earth. The physical and the spiritual are combined in a concentrated event. Heaven has come to earth. Earth is heaven. This central claim of Christian faith is a core confession of believing hearts and a powerful promise of God through which the world of our experience may be recreated and beloved places may be discovered and built. The final stanza of Wilbur's poem is,

> But now, as at the ending,
> The low is lifted high;
> The stars shall bend their voices,

And every stone shall cry.
And every stone shall cry
In praises of the child
By whose descent among us
The worlds are reconciled.[5]

When "worlds" of one kind and another are reconciled, there is peace. *Peace* means more than the cessation of conflict; from its Hebrew root, *shalom,* it means that all things are properly placed. When the angels exited the shepherd's world they sang "peace on earth." Heaven and earth are joined. A bifurcated universe, the spiritual separated from the physical, has been healed through the Word of God. A place is beloved—things and persons are properly placed in it—when words that name it as such are spoken.

Good Words

Benedictions (good words) go with worshipers when they leave a sanctuary full of words and sacramental meaning for secular worlds beyond it. The benediction is meant to go with them as a blessing, bringing the possibility that nearly every place could be or could *become* beloved, if only the inhabitants speak with authority words that claim and sanctify it.

Words bear the spirit. The roots of the biblical terms for spirit are members of a lexical family that includes wind, breath, soul, and life. The breath of God sweeps over the dark, formless void as a living breath in which God said, "'Let there be light'; and there was light" (Genesis 1:2–3). The power to form and to shape is the power of the imagination. The power to create a beloved place is the power to imagine it and then to name it so. A good, safe place in which to live and grow is a basic human need from birth onward to death. Providing places in which infants and young children are safe and cared for is an adult responsibility.

The Crèche

The French word *crèche* refers to a public nursery which in earlier times provided care for the infants of poor women. The public nursery of popular Christmas crèche scenes, seen every holiday season at church altars, in public places as well as in private living rooms and under Christmas trees, is an icon of Luke's narration of the Lord's humble and exposed birth in blatant, if temporary, poverty. The disarming attraction of this imaginary situation holds our interest. We want to see this thing, as the shepherds saw it. We want to help and honor the one lying there, as the wise men did. As was pointed out in the last chapter, life-finding-shelter attracts our attention. An emergency assembly of people in an unguarded and exposed setting catches the eyes of rescuers and defenders, in the same way it catches the eyes of predators and bandits. Emily Dickinson's poem "I Know Some Lonely Houses" begins,

> I know some lonely houses off the road
> A robber'd like the look of—

The familiar Christmas crèche—an undefended, miserable story-scene—is the ubiquitous holiday place definer. In garish suburban light displays, on lonely, snow-driven farmyards, in desert churchyards and department store windows, the nativity scene stakes a claim on the property around it.

In some communities, seasonal nativity scenes appear in public places a month or so after the end of the American election season, occupying the same prominent pieces of ground as political campaign posters. Evangelical campaign messages call for putting the incumbent back into the White House, then call for putting Jesus Christ back into Christmas. A facile preacher—not to mention a clever editorial writer or a perceptive social scientist—could draw out themes of election, outreach, birthright, and so on from these two seasonal lawn appointments. For the purpose of the present study, the nativity scene is more than a campaign sign for Christian evangelism. The Christmas nativity is a familiar public icon of faith, second only to the cross, and a poetic image containing latent emotion and collective human memory.

The general shape of the nativity scene often is a simple shelter, reminding us of the archetype of the isolated, ethically valorous peasant hut.

The Peasant Hut

The simple peasant hut is an attractive structure. Because the hospitality of poverty is rich, such a house seems to beckon a "welcome" without formality of introduction. The lost soul or the traveler might expect to be taken into such a place. Even the social scientist, professionally curious about those who live simple lives in a complex world, would expect to be welcomed and satisfied with data and answers to his or her questions. While the stable of Bethlehem is, in idealized form and imaginary renditions, a more or less isolated peasant hut, even children's illustrated Bibles point out that domestic animal shelters of first-century dwellings in ancient Palestine might have been corners of rooms adjacent to human sleeping quarters. A social-science commentary on the gospels states succinctly a reconstruction of such a residence:

> Peasant houses normally had only one room, though sometimes a guest room would have been attached. The family usually occupied one end of the main room and the animals the other. The manger was located in between. The manger would have been the normal place for peasant births, with the women of the house assisting.[6]

A visit to a home in rural native cultures in many parts of the world today might show a living arrangement in which the boundaries between human and animal habitation are fluid. The point, for the purposes of this book, is that the imagination might "design" other compact shelters to illustrate the birth of Jesus. However historians reconstruct the scene, the Christian imagination fills out the bare description of Jesus' birth scene primarily by identifying with the characters— sympathizing with Mary and with the baby in light of the residents' apparent failure to do so, for example—and by setting the stable in isolated relief against the night.

The family is outcast. Their open-air huddle is austere. Imagined from the perspective of time and distance—thousands of years and thousands of miles—the stable is the image of the peasant's hut, which, according to Bachelard, has deep emotional resonance in what he calls the "daydream of primitiveness" and of splendid, isolated refuge: "When we are lost in darkness and see a distant glimmer of light, who does not dream of a thatched cottage or, to go more deeply still into legend, of a hermit's hut?"[7] The hut, according to Bachelard, isolated and far from the congestion and commerce of population centers, is a primitive element in the human imagination, related to one's childhood home and to what might be a common childhood dream of primitiveness: "in the family sitting room, a dreamer of refuges dreams of a hut, of a nest, or of nooks and corners in which to hide away, like an animal in his hole."[8] A young boy's daydream of the splendid isolation of a cabin in the woods is a shade of the layered attractiveness of the Bethlehem stable. The stable is set in our imaginations as a distant event that happened long ago, without neighboring houses or distinguishing features.

The imagination isolates the Bethlehem stable so that everyone who hears the story may step forward and be part of the scene, a neighbor next door or a delighted visitor. The legendary star of Bethlehem in Matthew's Gospel, outstanding in the night sky and leading the wise men to Jesus' birthplace, corresponds as an isolated point of light in the night sky to the lonely location of Jesus' birth on the ground in Bethlehem. If the attraction of the scene lies in the dreams of isolation and of primitiveness then, as Bachelard writes, "in the land of legend, there exists no adjoining hut."[9]

The Spirit House

In some countries of the world, Thailand for example, people put up miniature dwellings for spirits. Introducing a photo essay of sacred spaces, architect Elizabeth Padjen writes that "the construction of these 'spirit houses' is an ancient practice rooted in animism, which continues in Thailand despite the adoption of other religions."[10] She notes that Christian churches are larger-scale spirit houses, built for the inhabitation of human beings; furthermore, sometimes these buildings are as distinctive as features of a culture and of a regional landscape as their miniature counterparts. For example, early Congregational meetinghouses, built in the northeast United States, gradually were replaced in the eighteenth and nineteenth centuries by "the most enduring symbol of New England: the white wooden church." These were constructed, and still stand, in an "enormous variety of styles: Federalist, Greek Revival, Gothic Revival, Victorian," each one of them designed and constructed as a spirit house, a place to shelter and nurture the spirit of their congregations, their communities, and their regions.

"Spirit house" fits as a description of other places we build for the investment of our personal time and our deepest concerns. These include but are not limited to houses of worship and houses for families to live in, to clubhouses and playhouses. Each of these might provide spaces for the exercising of our spirits and for the preservation of memory and hope.

Native Alaskans have a tradition of constructing spirit houses for their homes: composite artworks that interpret a family's history by representing individual family members as well as formative family events. Bethlehem nativity scenes, appearing in churches and homes, might be called Christian spirit houses. The small, stylized dwellings shelter Jesus and his mother, the two figures who embody the spirit of the Christian faith. In a Christian congregation or a Christian household, Mary, Jesus, and the supporting characters of nativity scenes represent the spiritual heritage and a lineage of faith.

All the spirit houses we have mentioned testify to the human belief that life can be temporarily ordered and contained. Constructing places in which to hold holy things and events is a well-known religious impulse, but the "building" of a holy place is a tricky project. Sometimes even before the corners are measured, the foundations laid, and the walls raised on a construction project meant to contain God, the divine spirit absconds. For example, when Jesus was transfigured on the mountain, Peter wanted to preserve the moment by building temporary shelters for Jesus, Moses, and Elijah.[11] A voice from heaven names Jesus as the son of God and seems not to allow localized corralling of holy events or characters. As Solomon prayed, "Will God indeed dwell on the earth? Even heaven and the highest heaven cannot contain you, much less this house that I have built!" (1 Kings 8:27). A nineteenth-century Christian hymn echoes this bittersweet observation:

> Not in our temples made with hands
> God, the Almighty, is dwelling;
> High in the heav'ns his temple stands,
> All earthly temples excelling.[12]

The Peaceful Place

Perhaps more than any other quality, *peace* is associated with a beloved place. Robert Frost's poem "The Death of the Hired Man" includes these lines of dialogue:

> "Home is the place where, when you have to go there,
> They have to take you in."
> "I should have called it
> Something you somehow haven't to deserve."[13]

That peace may not be an Edenic garden paradise of low-hanging fruit and slow-motion pleasures. The peace resulting from the reconciliation of worlds may result from a battle, or it may portend a battle to come. When the children of Israel arrived in Canaan, or when Jesus announced the kingdom of God, disruption of the status quo followed. When a person or thing comes to or returns to its proper place, its shalom, other residents or interlopers might be displaced. Painful adjustments might be required. The establishment of the peace of a place might entail uncomfortable justice. Refugees, for example, forced to flee their homes and the places they love, often are at the mercy of political, military, and economic forces. Places we love sometimes stand in the line of fire or in the eye of a storm. As William Percy wrote in his hymn "They Cast Their Nets in Galilee":

> The peace of God, it is no peace,
> But strife closed in the sod.
> Yet, let us pray for but one thing:
> The marv'lous peace of God.

The stones crying out along Jesus' way into Jerusalem announce his crucifixion and further reconciliations of life and death, of heaven and hell.

A Sabbath House

The third commandment says, "Observe the sabbath day and keep it holy." The law from the book of Deuteronomy continues in these words:

Six days you shall labor and do all your work. But
the seventh day is a sabbath to the LORD your God;
you shall not do any work—you, or your son or your
daughter, or your male or female slave, or your ox or
your donkey, or any of your livestock, or the resident
alien in your towns.

(DEUTERONOMY 5:13–14)

Rest for working animals—by name the ox and the donkey—is
a plank of God's covenant law with Israel. A day free of work
is commanded so that members of households may rest.
Included in the command, after human residents, are beasts
of burden as well as visitors. The Bethlehem nativity scene may
be looked at as a house of rest and a public sabbath moment.

For Martin Luther, a person, place, or thing becomes
holy through its relation with and connection to God's word.
Therefore, keeping the sabbath holy means attending to God's
word.[14] To Luther, the sanctifying of time, which the sabbath
command enjoins, happens whenever God's word is taught,
preached, heard, read, and pondered. God's word, for Luther,
is a living thing. The word of God is written in the text of the
scripture, tasted and touched in bread, wine, and water, and
known in the life of Jesus, beginning at the story of his birth.
In a Christmas sermon on the nativity, Luther wrote,

Look at the Child, knowing nothing. Yet all that is
belongs to him, that your conscience should not fear
but take comfort in him. Doubt nothing. To me there
is no greater consolation given to mankind than this,
that Christ became man, a child, a babe, playing in

the lap and at the breasts of his most gracious mother. Who is there whom this sight would not comfort? Now is overcome the power of sin, death, hell, conscience, and guilt, if you come to this gurgling Babe and believe that he is come, not to judge you, but to save.[15]

So, following Luther, sabbath rest means a relation to God's word. The sabbath may not be a day of the week. The segment of sabbath is time in relation to God's eternal word, so true sabbath rest comes from a relation to God's word, no matter the day of the week or the hour of the day. To Luther and to many other Christians, Jesus is the Word of God incarnate. In terms of the nativity scene, all the characters are in place in relation to the baby. As they gather around him, they keep a sabbath moment. Even the animals participate in the "rest" given by God and received through faith. This sabbath rest is related to salvation. The angels told the shepherds that the baby Jesus was the savior, the chosen one of God and the Lord. Around him life is refreshed, renewed, and redeemed. The sabbath is a holy "place" in time. Keeping a sabbath, by relating to God's word, may hallow places in physical space as well.

The Place of Animals

Nativity scenes, from magnificent sixteenth-century altarpieces to illuminated plastic ornaments on American front lawns, normally represent baby Jesus in the manger surrounded by Mary, Joseph, shepherds, wise men, angels, and animals. The presence of domesticated animals often is a mark of a beloved place. Pets may be the only company in an otherwise lonely house. A medieval Latin hymn includes the lines "Ox and ass before him bow" and "Now ye need not fear the grave; Jesus Christ was born to save."[16] Along with sheep, which fit the scene because they would naturally accompany the shepherds, most nativity depictions and installations throughout Christian centuries have included an ox, a donkey, and occasionally a dove.

The dove is known in the Bible as the harbinger of the end of the Flood,[17] as the form of the sacrifice prescribed in Leviticus for the purifying of the mother after childbirth,[18] and as the form of the Holy Spirit descending on Jesus.[19] The dove is the sign of blessing, reconciliation, and forgiveness and therefore is a symbol of peace in the Hebraic sense of shalom, in which people, things, and spaces are in proper in relation to other people, things, and spaces, and to God. The spiritual equilibrium is a sabbath ideal that may only be glimpsed and never realized fully.

Matthew and Luke do not mention an ox or a donkey, but historian Jeremy Wood writes that in some examples of very early Christian depictions of the nativity (from the fifth and sixth centuries), these two animals were more prominent figures even than Mary and Joseph. Medieval biblical legends filled in reasons beyond the biblical record for the presence of the ox and the donkey. For example, the donkey was Mary's transportation on the trip from Nazareth to Bethlehem, and Joseph brought an ox to help pay the Roman tax.[20] The presence of the animals under the shelter of the stable increases human fascination with the scene, illustrates biblical interest and sabbath concern for them, and completes an array of living things that naturally might be part of a single household.

Up until our present time, animals and people lived together. In urban living arrangements, a cat, dog, or goldfish might be the lonely representative of an older, rural way of life known by the ancestors of each city dweller. The manger scene in which animals and human beings live together in a small space might strike a resonant chord in contemporary people in much the same way that stray notes of wolfen instinct occasionally are struck in the brains of well-trimmed poodles and schnauzers.

In some of her poems, Vassar Miller identifies deeply with animals. They appear to be at home and at peace wherever they are, and they do not ponder their own deaths. She writes in her poem "Old Dog":

> Your shadow
> is death, old dog,
> yet you lie down beside it
>
> as trusting
> as a young pup
> sleeping beside its mother.[21]

Miller's poem "Carol of Brother Ass" is an imaginative appropriation of the story of Jesus' birth. In it the poet takes that story into her own body, suggesting that one's spiritual heart is a beloved place. The title of the poem reminds the reader of St. Francis, who identified with animals as fellow creatures of the earth. The donkey is a non-verbal, immediate receptor and conductor of the wonder and aching tragedy of the nativity. Eventual death is implied in every birth announcement. The poet, who possesses words and songs, stands with the donkey without denying the special perspective that her imagination and words provide. The poet imagines *herself* as the stable, the shelter around the nativity. The spiritual theology behind the poem is a piece of the gospel that often slips away from us as we meander and wend our way through life: The world is a beloved place and the Bethlehem of one's heart may be the setting of a great story, allowing one to be at home anyplace the word is heard and memory is alive:

> In the barnyard of my bone
> Let the animals kneel down—
> Neither ecstasy nor anger,
> Wrath nor mildness need hide longer,
> On the branching veins together
> Dove may sing with hawk her brother.
>
> Let the river of my blood
> Turned by star to golden flood
> Be the wholesome radiance
> Where the subtle fish may dance,
> Where the only bait to bite
> Dangles from the lures of light.
>
> Let the deep angelic strain
> Pierce the hollows of my brain;
> Struck for want of better bell,
> Every nerve grow musical;
> Make my thews and sinews hum
> And my tautened skin a drum.
>
> Bend, astonished, haughty head
> Ringing with the shepherds' tread;
> Heart, suspended, rib to rib,
> Rock the Christ Child in your crib,
> Till so hidden, Love afresh
> Lovely walks the world in flesh.[22]

Animals, calm companions and partners to haunted humans, may in loyalty stand by in any surrounding shelter. Humans project hopes and fears: future failure and the hope of transformation, even rebirth. The "hardest" lines of thought and imagination—and the least romantic—see the nativity as a serious story of life and death, a battle in a war fought within each human heart. When, as Vassar Miller writes, "Love afresh / Lovely walks the world in flesh," she knows that this means trouble. Love offered is love rejected. Love alive is love crucified. The final meditation of this chapter imagines the roof over the nativity as a chamber of disturbance, a vault of upheaval. The cave is a tomb of stone, a robber's lair, a fallout shelter.

Robert Southwell, a sixteenth-century Jesuit priest who served as a Catholic missionary in the dangerous territory of Protestant England, wrote vivid and devotional Christian poems. His "New Heaven, New Warre" sees the incarnation not as a placid tableau but as a paramilitary occupation of enemy territory:

> This little Babe so few dayes olde,
> Is come to ryfle Satans folde;
> All hell doth at his presence quake,
> Though he himselfe for cold doe shake:
> For in this weake unarmed wise,
> The gates of hell he will surprise.

To Southwell, the nativity scene is an encampment from which the battle for souls will be launched and directed:

> His Campe is pitched in a stall,
> His bulwark but a broken wall:

The Crib his trench, hay stalks his stakes,
Of Sheepheards he his Muster makes . . .²³

Based on the physical peril of his own vocational service to
the Catholic Church, in an environment in which Catholic
devotion could be punished by death, the beloved place of
Southwell's nativity of Jesus is a guerrilla outpost. A field-
command center of inspiration, strategy, leadership—as well
as the home to be defended—Southwell's nativity is a bivouac
for the prosecution of spiritual warfare, the deciding battle of
which will come at the end of this baby's life.

Southwell and the other poets mentioned in this chapter—
Vassar Miller and Richard Wilbur—are all struck by this fact
of life: the Baby Jesus, born in Bethlehem, will die someday. If
this is the Son of God, born in Bethlehem of Judea in the reign
of Augustus, some day and in some place, the Son of God
will die. The facing of death will be the final battle in the war,
but how will this story be told and retold? The nativity of the
Son of God is an alien visit and a dubious curiosity unless one
ponders the disturbing thought that this newborn child of the
earth will be subject to death. Therefore the Christian imagination cannot see Bethlehem without seeing Calvary overlaid
on it: the cross in the beams of the stable or the mausoleum
over the manger. Southwell imagined this eventuality starkly.
The baby is going to face the grave and the angels of darkness:
"The gates of hell he will surprise."

The Cave

Graves in the ancient Syro-Palestinian world often were tomb-
caves in the limestone hills. Living animals and groups of
people found shelter in similar caves and served people in life

and in death. Historians tell us that the "stable" that sheltered baby Jesus and his attendants might be accurately imagined as a hillside cave. This is a further—and not as often explicated—identification of Jesus' birth with his death: If we imagine a grave as an ancient cave-tomb, such as we may picture in our imaginations from the Easter story, the cavern of Jesus' birth begins to resemble the stone-sealed tomb of his death. The elementary but fundamental point connecting birth to death and death to birth could be created in a couplet ending with full rhymes: womb and tomb, cave and grave. These life and death images are the openings and endings of every human story and the basis for Christian interpretation of original and ultimate meaning.

A poem titled "The Cave," by contemporary poet David Brendan Hopes, packages some of the images and themes of our discussion so far: the manger as a rock supporting life; the water of birth and life; a shelter, a cave, to which visitors bring golden gifts and which "holds" the explorer of the imagination as a home place.

> We entered from the north.
> There were two sounds: water, bees.
> There was one engorging dark.
> The water came both from outside
> and from farther down,
> splashing, flowing. The bees
> moled in from the field above,
> laid down their honey in live rock
> where cold and enemies never come.
> We had not seen them in the field,
> not seen them dropping, laden,

where there grew no flower.
We heard them droning on the roof,
the sound, if we did not keep our
thoughts on edge, like the cave
speaking one syllable, invariable, continuous.
It was purple beyond the reach of our lamps.
We aimed the flashlights out, pretending
to look for blocks or ways,
but looking at the purple,
purple like the robe of someone leading us
just out of sight.
At what seemed the bottom was a clear pool
shallow over pebbles. I dipped my hand in.
Under the water I was the color of the stones,
pale, clean. At that moment
I was frightened, and at home.[24]

One can read this poem as a kind of allegory of the story of
Jesus' life without claiming that this is what the poet "meant."
After all, a poem stands as an artifact on the page. A good or
great poem might open up to numerous reading approaches.
Stones, caves, the color purple, and a number of other theologically suggestive objects and qualities might mean different
things to other readers; certainly, too, the surface reading of
a narrative poem such as this one, in which rocks and water
simply are rocks and water, is always before us, just as the
surface of the world is always before us. However, scientists,
children, poets, artists, and saints see stories and hear music
beneath and above the surface of things. Faith-minded readers often can read sacred stories from a compelling tale or
poem told in terms of the natural world.

The poem begins with spelunkers entering from the north. Readers of Luke's nativity come down from the north, traveling with the holy family from Nazareth to Bethlehem. The poet's specification of the direction from which the bees come may suggest to some readers a spiritual exploration downward and, of course, inward.

Bees entering the cave from the surrounding fields to lay their treasure on the ledges and walls of the living rock are like the shepherds coming to offer their praise, and like Matthew's gift-bearing wise men, attracted to the sheltering dark. The purple that backdrops the scene fascinates the explorers and seems to lead them. This is a royal ribbon of the color that draws the church through Advent to the birth of the king, and through Lent to the enthronement of the King Jesus on the cross, and on to the rebirth of the world in the resurrection.

Water and rock are the natural repositories of memory. Each contains an eternal aspect. Water is life itself. It runs and disappears, streams away, returns and collects in rivulets, channels, and pools. Bachelard wrote:

> I can't sit beside a brook without falling into a deep reverie, without seeing once again my happiness. . . . The stream doesn't have to be ours; the water doesn't have to be ours. The anonymous water knows all my secrets. And the same memory issues from every spring.[25]

Rock—in monuments, artifacts, and natural formations— contains memory condensed. Bachelard wrote that "man is born of rock."[26] Archaeologists and historians read a historical script from rubble and pieces of rock. Strolling through a city made of rock—such as the Old City of Jerusalem—one can almost hear an ancient, layered chorus of history emanating from massive stone walls. The blocks represent new construction on top of the work of ancient artisans. Rock, especially rock cut and shaped by human hands, is packed with memory and information. If human voices—carrying their often-unreliable interpretation of history and of current events—are silenced, as Wilbur's poem has it, memory-infused stones would cry out in praise and alarm (cf. Luke 19:39–40). Chapter Four, under the heading of Bethlehem as Joseph's ancestral town, returns to consideration of a cave, a shelter of stone, which today commemorates the birth of Jesus: the grotto at the center of the Church of the Nativity in Bethlehem.

I went to heaven.
'Twas a small town,
Lit with a ruby,
Lathed with down.

EMILY DICKINSON (1830–1886)

It is a mad thing, to be alive. Villages exist to moderate this
madness—to hide it from children, to bottle it for private
use, to smooth its imperatives into habits, to protect us from
the darkness without and the darkness within.

JOHN UPDIKE (B. 1932), *VILLAGES*

I miss Mayberry
Sitting on the porch drinking ice cold Cherry Coke
Where everything is black and white.

ARLOS SMITH, "MAYBERRY"

≡ *Three*

BETHLEHEM

IT SHOULD BE ADMITTED, even in this book about our love of place, that most Americans are, according to philosopher Deborah Tall,

> awash in a landscape of mobility that eschews connections to particular plots, has no need or desire for great distinctions between places, and is essentially utilitarian about the land, often lacking environmental conscience. Place has come to mean proximity to highways, shopping and year-round recreation, rather than natural situation or indigenous character.[1]

However, Tall continues, many of us are not satisfied with this slippery, rootless way of living in relation to places: "Yet we remain caught between nostalgia for place in its traditional sense and cool detachment, between a sense of responsibility for the land and the freedom of indifference."

This chapter sails against the current of American root-lessness. We will look at Bethlehem, the "little town" of Christmas devotion, and for contrast and comparison, set it against the American mythology of wholesome small towns with old-fashioned Main Streets. Thoughts and analysis will be stretched back and forth between these two communities, real and idealized, Bethlehem of Judea (today Bethlehem of the Israeli-occupied West Bank of the Jordan River) and Springfield, Minnesota (a small town on the Minnesota prairie). These two towns together will show aspects of the same general dream of a beloved place.

Where Two or Three Are Gathered

There was no place for Mary and Joseph in the inn, so the baby was born and laid in a manger, a place that may register in our minds' eyes as inappropriate. Still we imagine that through the mother's instinct and creativity a birthplace—a temporary nest of straw—was found and created for her child. The Bethlehem nativity scene, with the manger as its center, normally is marked by a rough structure representing a stable. More important, however, are the people huddled there, their attention focused on the central figure. These characters recall the event and define the place. As an adult, Jesus articulated this important principle of a beloved place: "For where two or three are gathered in my name, I am there among them" (Matthew 18:20).

On a drizzly, warm spring night, as my oldest son and I drove home from an evening outing to the Home Depot store, we slowed our Volkswagen behind a few cars stopped in front of St. Zepherin's Catholic Church. An elderly man—known to area shelters for the homeless—was lying in the road. Having drunk too much, he had careened in front of a car and lost control of his bicycle on the slippery pavement. He lay there on the side of the road, shivering under the plaid stadium blanket that someone had spread over him and claiming that he had been hit by the car even as he pleaded to be taken home.

Before the police arrived, cars crept by in the rain, their drivers peering out through the streetlights at the small huddle of people forming a shield around the man on the ground. These included the driver of the car who had allegedly struck the bicyclist, a woman and her dog, another driver who held his jacket like an awning over the man on the ground, and me. Looking back on this temporary encampment in front of the church I am reminded of a nativity scene: an awkward assembly defining a place, drawing the attention of passersby, diverting traffic and hallowing the ground around a child of the earth.

Sometimes, then, it is certain people who define most closely the places we love. These people might crowd in to an emergency or an accident like the one described above. They might live only in the minds and memories of mobile Americans who move from place to place in search of a better life.

A Spiritual Community

In the collective memory of ancient Israel there exists a tribal community, a nomadic band moving through the desert to a promised land, led by God's Spirit. There is as well an aching love of places never seen by that band of God's children, a nostalgia, as it were, for a city of peace. That mobile community's exoduses and exiles—their extended displacements—are dynamic metaphors that expand and enliven the biblical and communal notions of a beloved place. The wanderer, the seeker, the expatriate might love the place from which he is absent, or the place he has not yet attained, more than a long-time resident loves it.

Christian theology relies on an active Holy Spirit to enliven faith in people, to equip a congregation for service in community, to sanctify a place, to make a house a home. The spirits of ancestors who once lived in a certain town or neighborhood, set against a remembered landscape or a recalled building, may haunt or bless a place for the living. How many people have lived restlessly and uncomfortably in a strange town or a foreign land only to return home to familiar objects, sights, and routines that contain memories of family? The Psalmist wrote, "How could we sing the LORD's song in a foreign land?" (137:4).

Most people need a spiritual community—real or imagined—and familiar touchstones to which they might return. The Apostles' Creed recalls the great spiritual community of the living and the dead, which is known as the "communion of saints." As Christians move through their lives, from year to year and house to house, their spiritual communities may accompany them. Creeds and church teachings, hymns and scripture equip the minds and the hearts of people on the move in the world. Ghosts of memory haunt our days and nights and soothe our souls. Familiar touchstones, such as recalled landscapes, objects, stories, or certain other people who stand in extraordinary relation to ourselves, may hold our hearts and minds "in place" even in exile or on a journey.

The Memory of Parents

The present chapter and the one that follows are inspired by two of the featured attendants in the nativity scene, Joseph and Mary. Each one will guide our thoughts into different aspects of places we love. Through meditations on the place of Joseph we will consider the meaning of a small town, especially in our American imaginations. Luke tells us that Joseph and Mary went to Bethlehem because it was Joseph's ancestral town. Joseph was a descendant of the great king, David, and Bethlehem was the birthplace of David. Then, in the next chapter, Mary will guide us into thoughts of a mother's love that continues to bless even an adult child's place with gifts of words.

O Little Town

Historians estimate that in the days about which Luke was writing, Bethlehem was a hamlet of a few hundred people. Today there are more than forty thousand residents of the small city of Bethlehem. Like Jerusalem (also known in the Bible as the City of David), Bethlehem is a place saturated with eons of compacted history and emotion. Its auras and influences infuse the whole world. If our own homes and rooms are filled with the spirits of our families and our own life stories, Bethlehem is alive with the ghosts of many ages of human life.

Speaking about Bethlehem in an interview, novelist Reynolds Price said:

> You can also see how it's no accident that people have been in a semi-insane contention for the rights to this place forever, for as long as we can remember in human history. There is something truly sacred about the place that makes you see how it can drive people almost crazy.[2]

A hundred years or so before Price visited Bethlehem, another traveler, the Reverend Phillips Brooks, walked the streets of the town as a Christian pilgrim. A year or so after Brooks returned from his pilgrimage, full of impressions and inspiration of that exotic yet strangely familiar place, he collaborated with his church's organist, Lewis Henry Redner, to compose a carol for their church's Sunday school Christmas program. This children's hymn, "O Little Town of Bethlehem," became a holiday standard for people of all ages. Bethlehem, the hometown of our imaginations, is an unreal, idealized village that we may all claim and "return to" as we sing,

O little town of Bethlehem,
How still we see thee lie!
Above thy deep and dreamless sleep,
The silent stars go by.
Yet in thy dark streets shineth
The everlasting light.
The hopes and fears of all the years
Are met in thee tonight.

What Reynolds Price said directly about Bethlehem in that interview is what Brooks wrote with pastoral gentleness in his hymn text: "the hopes and fears of all the years" are met in "the little town" of Bethlehem. Layered and condensed hopes, dreams, ambitions, disappointments, the daily rounds of generations, and eons of human life invested there, remain through the years in a beloved place. This is why the tragedy of homelessness, the flight of refugees, and the plight of orphans are so poignant and painful. The loss of a place in which one can feel rooted and attached is a dear loss indeed.

Bethlehem on the West Bank

Bethlehem imagined is the hometown of Christians. People who pause to hear Luke's Gospel revere it. The center of the present, earthly city Bethlehem, in territory occupied by the Israeli military, is the Church of the Nativity in Manger Square. The center of the church is a grotto, a circular, subterranean chamber with a silver star on the ground surrounded above by fifteen lamps representing Christian denominations of the world. This is the precise point that "drives people crazy." The star is inscribed with the Latin words *Hic de Virgine Maria Jesus Christus natus est* (Here the Virgin Mary gave birth to Jesus Christ).

This grotto is a cave of rock with walls saturated with the personal stories, the hopes and fears, of countless generations. This dusty, gaudy church—to many Western eyes bizarrely appointed—is a spiritual anchor point of earth. G. K. Chesterton wrote of it: "In the place where he was homeless, all men are at home."

The aspirations and conflicts of peoples and nations have been carried to Bethlehem by residents, occupiers, pilgrims, and tourists. Today the Church of the Nativity and Bethlehem around it are occupied by the Israeli military. Palestinian refugee camps, each with thousands of inhabitants, spread out from the town. The beloved town of Bethlehem is part of a long and bitter conflict between Israelis and Palestinians.

Whose place is it? Whose home and whose "peace" should the little town of Bethlehem keep and support? The politics and brutal realities of the long-running dispute in the Holy Land must be acknowledged but cannot be examined thoroughly within the scope of this book. This conflict—simmering and raging on for generations—is more than a local dispute over land. It is a clash of cultures and regions of the world. The roots of the problem are fed from and continue to impinge on the histories of many nations and empires. However, hidden and buried in Bethlehem, that place of disagreement and violent passion, are the seeds of peace. Phillips Brooks's Christmas hymn offers the thought that Bethlehem, the world's hometown, trembling in a maelstrom of mistrust and hatred, of military occupation and seething resentment, somewhere and somehow contains a promise of peace.

Joseph's Town

Americans who have no experience of the present city of Bethlehem, in Palestine, five miles south of Jerusalem, may find that when they sing "O Little Town of Bethlehem" their minds flash to an idealized small town. It is perhaps the Midwestern or Southern or quaint New England town of their grandparents or great-grandparents, the product, at least in part, of an American village mythology. Yi-Fu Tuan wrote that "the dominant myths of America are nonurban. They are often antiurban."[3] In *Habits of the Heart: Individualism and Commitment in American Life*, Robert Bellah emphasized how deeply nostalgia for life in a small town persists among the American citizens he and the other editors interviewed:

> The erosion of meaning and coherence in our lives is not something Americans desire. Indeed, the profound yearning for the idealized small town that we found among most of the people we talked to is a yearning for just such meaning and coherence.[4]

The loss of the small town—such as the kind we know in
Thornton Wilder's Grover's Corners and Andy Griffith's Mayberry, the quintessential hometown, as the spiritual center of
American life—is felt as corporate grief, homesickness for a
village of our own, a community of belonging, a strong tribe,
or a successful team of which we might be contributing members. Yi-Fu Tuan wrote:

> Just as the pretense "love for humanity" arouses our
> suspicion, so "love of place" rings false when it is
> claimed for a large territory. A compact size scaled
> down to man's biologic needs and sense-bound
> capacities seems necessary. In addition, a people can
> more readily identify with an area if it appears to be
> a natural unit. Affection cannot be spread over an
> empire. . . .[5]

My Father's Town

One of the cards I received after my father's death included a
handwritten note that read in part, "When your father dies,
you can no longer go 'home.'" The card was written by a man
of my father's generation who, like my father, grew up in rural Minnesota. The words mean to me that the father's presence, knowledge, discipline, and love for his family and for his
family's place in the world stake out an original beloved place.
At the father's death, the son or daughter's way back into that
certain and particular beloved place of childhood is restricted,
rerouted, or blocked entirely.

Another old friend, speaking to me a few days after my
father's funeral, said, "When a man's father dies, it's like an

earthquake. The ground under you shifts." The features of a beloved place are rearranged. The landscape has changed, new plots of land to be loved appear where the old ones have crumbled and buckled into the earth. Grief for what was lost remains even as new beloved places appear.

My father was born in 1939, in a small town in northern Minnesota, to second-generation Scandinavian immigrant parents. His town of less than two thousand residents, Ada, Minnesota, was the Norman County seat. His father owned and operated a feed and fertilizer business that served farmers of the Red River Valley, where sections of farmland are stitched together as flat as a quilt spread on a table, out to the Dakota prairies.

In the 1940s the small American town was already threatened as a paragon of American life. The farm economy was changing. Young people were streaming to the cities for choices and opportunities. My father and mother were high school sweethearts. He was the quarterback on the six-man football team and she was the homecoming queen. After college and a stint in the Navy in California they moved to another, slightly larger, town on the prairie, two hundred miles south of Ada. This move crossed a continental divide. The Red River, a feature of my father's childhood, flows north to Lake Winnipeg and the Hudson Bay. The Cottonwood and the Minnesota, the rivers of my childhood, flow south.

For a year in Springfield he taught vocational agriculture to high school students. He must have been a lot like the farm boys with whom he was penned up in the classroom: impatient and independent, bucking to get outdoors and away from books and tests. Even though he got to know those boys and their families, and was able to visit them on their farms, he was temperamentally unsuited to classroom teaching. So after a year or two of teaching he went to work as a nutritionist for the feed company in town. He worked his way up to sales manager and then to general manager and vice president of what was by then a subsidiary of a larger agribusiness conglomerate.

The American Small Town

During the early years of my parents' life in Springfield, as my brothers and I were born, Springfield was still flush with the small-town vitality of the first half of the century. Before the Great Depression, 60 percent of the American population lived in small towns and on farms around them, but even in the decade prior to the Depression, developing technology was changing economic and social patterns of the country and writers such as Sinclair Lewis and Sherwood Anderson began a literary revolt against American village life. As these writers criticized the human culture of small towns, census takers noted a pattern of movement out of rural areas to urban centers. As early as the first quarter of the twentieth century, it was clear that the future belonged to the cities. Electric lights, the automobile, the telephone, every further convenience and advancement drove more and more people to urban economic and social centers:

> Working its way east, decline started to crisscross small-town America in the 1920s, conveyed by the automobiles that took rural citizens, body and mind, out of their own small villages to nearby towns and cities. Decline became generalized in succeeding decades,

as youth in ever greater numbers left farm and town, county bank assets accumulated in regional centers, and small service centers served fewer with less. By the 1990 census, even the most ardent boosters were stymied in their attempts to deny this exodus and the pessimistic trends associated with it.[6]

Still, to a certain kind of independent person, the 1940s and 50s were prosperous and blessed decades in many small towns; in some cases towns retained that character for the next twenty years. While the children of the first part of the century were alive, the small town I grew up in seemed to maintain a spirit of healthy, community-based piety (six viable churches in a town of 2,500 residents), civic responsibility, school pride, and economic vigor. Neat and clean, tucked inside wide expanses of cropland that fed the world, the small town could still be a dreamscape, especially for a child from a secure family. The same kind of small town that Sinclair Lewis could so thoroughly pierce and deflate with social satire could be a comfortable hometown, enjoyed and valued by its residents and remembered with fondness by its scattered children.

The nostalgia that an urban man like Phillips Brooks felt for the "little town" was alive in Americans throughout the rapid cultural and economic changes of the twentieth century, and probably is not entirely absent from the American psyche today, early in the twenty-first century. In a 1993 essay the author and teacher Frank Conroy wrote with regret of the homogenization of the American landscape in which Pizza Huts, Midas Mufflers, and Wal-Marts stitch the country together. Lost, in Conroy's view, is the small town's Main Street, which, he wrote, was "a stabilizing, civilizing, intimate, communal experience":

> For a very long time it was the small towns that held the country together, that kept it from fragmenting as a result of its great centrifugal energies. If the first social unit was the family, then the second was the small town. Tens upon tens of thousands of them across the wide face of the land, as numerous as stars in the night sky, they provided the reference points for the moral sextant of the country. It was the towns, not the cities, that provided the underpinnings for the great American experiment.[7]

Conroy continues in a tone quite contrary to that of Sinclair Lewis, commenting that among citizens of small towns

> [T]here was a sense of communal responsibility, of taking care of one's own, that moved basic, hard-learned family values out into the larger framework of society. . . . In a sense, small towns were a dramatization of people's connection to the land, a constant reminder of our rootedness in physical nature.[8]

As the American city is surrounded by suburbs in which those who work in the city live, the small town is surrounded by a natural landscape. It is an oasis in the desert or a great ship sailing on the sea of the prairie grassland. The small Midwestern town is surrounded by farms and fields. My own hometown, Springfield, Minnesota, was established in the nineteenth century along the railroad line and near the banks of a shallow river. Daily all its residents have felt the effects of weather and seasonal change on the farmers and their operations around town.

Rooted in the Land

During my years in Springfield most of the town's residents worked at the brickyard, the air compressor factory, at the feed mill, or in the retail stores on Main Street. Others were service-providers and professionals: bankers, teachers, doctors, lawyers. But nearly everyone had roots of some kind in the land—if not direct roots, at least economic or social ties to people who had direct roots. Farm life was all around. The eyes of the citizens of town rested every day on the cultivated fields that changed from black to thin-then-lush green, and finally to dry autumn shades of yellow and brown.

Before I started elementary school, but within my memory, my father moved our family from a small house in town to a much larger place about a half-mile outside the city limits. The four-bedroom prairie house had been designed by a local architect for his retirement home, with room enough for his children and grandchildren to visit. But the Arizona sun eventually pulled the architect and his wife away from Minnesota, and my dad bought his house. With its thoughtful, open, high-ceilinged, one-story design, the house seemed to fit the fields and the wide sky around it. Set on a hill and surrounded by six acres of lawn and pasture, the place had plenty of room to keep sheep and board horses and, for one or two seasons, an old farmer's parade mules. There was room for my father's friend, Eddie Albertson, to plant a garden. There was room for a long rope swing from a maple tree as old as the town itself, and for a basketball court. There was room to plant a windbreak of pine trees, poplars, and honeysuckle. To the southeast and below the house was a view of the railroad tracks and three intersecting roads. Beyond the intersection, the Cottonwood River Valley wound its way to the Minnesota River, where it joined water running to the Mississippi's wide flow down to the Gulf of Mexico.

I wonder if my father moved us out of town because *he* needed the room: an arm's length away from the measured lots and streets of a small town and the measuring eyes of neighbors and acquaintances. Our parents' choices mark their children forever, but the children cannot fully understand the dreams and pressures by which the parents' made those choices. I know certainly that the home my father bought for his family was among the first places I loved. When my own boys were very young they stood on the bottom plank of the fence separating the lawn from the pasture and looked out over the river valley, counting the cars of the freight train as it passed below them, just as I used to do.

The Children's Town

In my own family's suburban world near Boston, my boys have good schools and lovely tree-lined streets. They have music and sports teams and highly motivated, politely competitive peers who live in homes managed by motivated and politely competitive parents. They are members of a small Christian congregation. Within their church, which someday they might look back on as their village, they have relationships with a few young people their age but with many more people their parents' and grandparents' ages. One thing my boys may be missing in their lives is the setting of roots "in physical nature" that Frank Conroy said small towns provide for those who reside in them.

Suburban gardening and landscape maintenance draw people into a relation with the natural world that does not quite fit the spirit of what Conroy meant by having *roots* in the land. Planting flowers and shrubs around a suburban Colonial and feeding songbirds in the backyard may be a move in the direction of having roots in the land. What Conroy meant by *roots* in physical nature, however, is not aesthetic appreciation of nature that is characteristic perhaps of a vacationer, a casual birder, or a Hummer driver "adventuring" in a national park. Conroy speaks instead of the roots of a *resident,* one who sees with eyes altered by his or her residency in a certain place, in an interdependent, working relationship with the land and with non-human creatures.

The Shepherds

Frank Conroy wrote that small towns held the country together, but the forces that hold small towns in place come from outside of town. The economic, social, and spiritual fields of energy flow into town from the farms and fields around it. The small town would have dissolved without the centripetal force of the land around it. The good life of the small town, remembered and imagined with nostalgia by some Americans, streamed in from the farms and fields that surrounded the small towns. Similarly the news of Jesus' birth was brought into Bethlehem from the fields on the outskirts of town. Our access as readers to the story of Jesus' birth is brought in through the shepherds.

Certainly shepherds were participants in physical nature, tending their sheep and steering them safely to the next grazing field, but were they members of the community or were they interlopers? Were they insiders or were they outsiders? The ambiguity of the shepherds' station in life is one of the poetic engines of the nativity story. These unsheltered outcasts are the invited guests. The shepherds, who occupied a low rung on the village class ladder (if indeed they were on a rung of the ladder at all)—without access to avenues of commerce or to halls of society—were the only invited guests. By their friendly and pastoral call on Mary, Joseph, and the baby, they brought their roots in physical nature into that harbor of heaven of the Bethlehem manger scene. The interchange and emotional duet between the angels and the shepherds lit up the sky above and the ground below, making *heaven and nature sing* together.

Through the centuries some artists, interpreting the nativity in painting and figures, have been bold enough to dislodge Joseph from his symmetrical position opposite Mary and to place him in the background with the shepherds. I imagine Joseph stepping out behind the walls of the birthing room with the shepherds. In a moment of Christmas reverie I imagine my father there with them too, talking together as dreamers rooted in the land would feel free to talk (though neither they nor he would ever think of themselves as dreamers) about the lack of water on the hills, the brazenness of the wolves in a dry season, the chop of the waves somewhere on a distant sea, the health of the flocks, and the moisture of the soil under their feet.

They who kept watch over their flocks by night, and my father who kept watch over his boys as we tromped along prairie

fence-lines hunting pheasants, are among the simple visionaries of the world. Relatively unbothered by trends of fashion
and the herds of the city, those who live in rural places might
have a freedom—if they can claim it—for what a Minnesota
essayist and fiction writer called "quiet and honest thought,"
an environment in which people might rediscover "the old joy
of quietly thinking about things."[9]

Hunting

Drawing on his rural roots, replanted around Springfield
through his teaching and his work in agribusiness, my father knew the names of the families that lived on the farms
around our town. This was an advantage in late fall during the
pheasant hunting season. Weekend afternoons in October
and November he would drive my brothers and me out on
the gravel roads, south and west of town, to hunt pheasants.
Near evening, when the walking part of the hunt was done
and the sun had not yet set to end the hunting day, we drove
home slowly, looking for pheasants in the ditches and the
edges of the fields as the birds moved to their night shelter. As
we drove along together we enjoyed—without saying a word
about it, of course—the contours of the fall fields and the
family farms set beside them with corn harvested from the
fields packed into bins and in good years piled on the ground.
My father was rooted in the land through pheasant hunting.
Hunting may train one's eyes to see and love an environment
including the non-human inhabitants who live in it on their
own terms.

By taking me hunting as a boy, my father gave me a window
on a particular prairie agricultural environment. Through that

window I developed as a young man what one scholar describes as "an emotional link" to the land. The emotional link—quite vivid to me then—meant that I looked for, and noticed with excitement, pheasants on the edge of a gravel road, or ducks on the river, geese circling a cornfield, or a Labrador retriever in the back of a pickup, its blaze-orange collar indicating that the animal was more than a family pet. The sights of these creatures in their proper environments, which I shared with them as a hunter, created an emotional attachment—what Conroy might have called roots in the land.

If I could tally all the birds my father bagged over the many years he enjoyed hunting, and divided them up against the hours he spent hunting, the hours would exceed the birds many times over. More often than not our hunting excursions ended without taking a bird or even taking a shot, but each hunt was a successful outing, another return to a mildly mysterious territory of wild things and to their places on the edges of a human environment.

Just over a year or so before my father died, while he was still able to get out on his own, he said to me in a phone conversation across the thousand miles between Springfield and Boston, "I've started to go out driving in the country in the evening." In my mind I went with him, enjoying the silence of the drive and light fading above the prairie farmland.

Light

As I recall with pleasure the experiences I had road hunting in the evening with my father, I remember the effects of fading light on the farmland. We never said we were going out driving for the sunsets, and we never went out for the sunsets. But sunsets on the prairie are often red and broad, and snow skies, especially in late fall, are a wool-blanket gray. This time of day under the prairie sky lays a sweet heaviness on the heart, especially when the evening spreads over the lonely lights from the farms along the road and in the distance.

Gaston Bachelard explores the primitive image of a single light from a house in the country. He writes that the image of a lamp glowing in the window of an isolated house "would have to be placed under one of the greatest of all theorems of the imagination of the world of light. . . . The lamp keeps vigil, therefore it is vigilant. And the narrower the ray of light, the more penetrating its vigilance."[10] The light on the tall post that illuminates the driveway for a farm family is an attractive, fluid image. To the imagination, the cluster of farm buildings is an ark, a yacht, or a cruise ship, afloat at safe distances from other vessels, on the black, blowing sea of the prairie.

Richard Wilbur's Christmas poem, the north star of this book, begins with these lines:

A stable lamp is lighted
whose glow shall wake the sky.

Here is a single light of high emotional and spiritual intensity. A stable lamp shining out on a dark night is, as Bachelard puts it, an image of the "valorization of the center of concentrated solitude." A piercing spiritual and poetic image, such a light draws the traveler to shelter, the pilgrim to contemplation, the monk to prayer, the child to a dream of refuge. The single light in an environment of rural darkness is an eye in the night. Richard Wilbur's poem's Christmas conceit of the stable lamp "waking the sky" is at once a primitive archetype, a useful poetic image, and a theological claim about the Christian doctrine of the Incarnation.

In an interview published in 1995, Wilbur said that his "rather solitary" childhood, on a farm in North Caldwell, New Jersey, trained his eyes to nature and turned him into "an observer of natural processes."[11] One can imagine the poet as a boy being aware of various forms of light on his farm. As a beam of light from an isolated lamp maintains a ray of hope in otherwise overwhelming darkness, Wilbur's imagined stable lamp in Bethlehem shines a metaphysical light in the otherwise overwhelming darkness of human nature and human history. As the words of the angels and the response of the shepherds make heaven and nature sing, the poet's stable lamp and Matthew's star, by which the wise men found their way to Bethlehem, complete a circuit of spiritual illumination.

Even the sparrow finds a home,
and the swallow a nest for herself
where she may lay her young . . .

PSALM 84:3

Immensity cloistered in thy dear womb,
Now leaves his well-beloved imprisonment,
There he hath made himself to his intent
Weak enough, now into our world to come;
But Oh, for thee, for him, hath th' Inn no room?
Yet lay him in this stall, and from the Orient,
Stars, and wisemen will travel to prevent
Th' effect of Herod's jealous general doom.
Seest thou, my Soul, with thy faith's eyes, how he
Which fills all place, yet none holds him, doth lie?
Was not his pity towards thee wondrous high,
That would have need to be pitied by thee?
Kiss him, and with him into Egypt go,
With his kind mother, who partakes thy woe.

JOHN DONNE (1573–1631), "NATIVITY"

Mary had a baby, aye Lord.
Mary had a baby, aye my Lord.
Mary had a baby, aye Lord.
The people keep a-comin'
And the train done gone.

AMERICAN FOLK SONG

≋ *Four*

MARY

*1*N HER POEM "Homecoming Blues," Vassar Miller seems to envy her dogs their unanxious outlook on life.

> My dogs who have already forgotten how much they
>   missed me
> say nothing either.
> And O O O O
> I wish I could call my mother
> or eat death like candy.

Animals such as the pets in this poem help define the places we love. This is as true of the Bethlehems of our collective and personal imaginations as it is of the actual homes in which we live. The ox and donkey of our nativity imaginations, the dogs and cats of our households, play important supporting roles. The same can be said of other people: they help define the places we love. The absence of the mother's voice, wished for in the poem above but for some reason unavailable to the poet, increases the loneliness of the room. Those central and well-known characters of the gospel nativity stories set the scene. Without the shepherds, the wise men, Mary, and, Joseph, the story would be lonely and much different from the one we recall by heart. The present chapter continues from the previous one, drawing inspiration from the people whose presence, in body or spirit, define places we love.

People we love may create beloved places independent of geographic location. Nearly any place—even an uncomfortable place—may be a place we love if the right person is present in it. This may seem a shallow interpretation of place, but the power to turn an ordinary place into a beloved place is a movable and transferable human magic. A couple or a family may move to a place unfamiliar to them, and there quickly form a bond with the place simply because they are there together. A family on vacation, away from work and regular routines, may grow attached to a place. The remarkable effect that relationships have on making places beloved can be seen in the book of Ruth. Speaking to her mother-in-law Naomi, Ruth says, with determination and affection:

> Where you go, I will go;
> > where you lodge, I will lodge;
> your people shall be my people,
> > and your God my God.
> Where you die, I will die—
> > there will I be buried. (Ruth 1:16–17)

In the Gospel of Luke, when Emperor Augustus called for a census, Joseph, who was related to Naomi through the royal ancestry of King David, went down to David's town of Bethlehem.[1] In Bethlehem Mary gave birth to a baby boy, and there created a new layer of memory in a beloved place for Israel and Mary's Christian descendants. Joseph followed the footsteps of his family and his ancestor King David down to Bethlehem. Mary followed Joseph because they were engaged. The Christian church follows both of them and joins the layered spiritual meanings of the natal scene.

The heavenly messengers of the meaning of the nativity are angels. The angels' earthly and earthy counterparts are the shepherds. Condensed biblical prophecy and extra-biblical legend that flowed into, and even now flow out of, this biblical event tumble out of the shepherds' mouths. Their words foreshadow preachers and commentators, learned scholars, spirit-drunk fools, artists, and scoffers, all of whom have had a lot to "say" about this event: the shepherds "made known what had been told them about this child" (Luke 2:17). The shepherds are the first historians and cultural critics: "and all who heard [them] were amazed at what the shepherds told them"; but Mary, the mother, keeps praise and identity, contradictory claims and biblical commentary uncritically in her heart of love: "Mary treasured all these words and pondered them in her heart" (Luke 2:19).

The mother's words, kept in graceful order safely within herself, are the theme of this chapter. She who bore the Word of God in her body keeps words of life in her heart. This chapter ponders, with Mary, the power of the word about and around her Son, Jesus, then meditates on the gift of words given by a mother to her grown children, living in a different place but still held in place in that mother's heart.

Creating a Place

Places we love are mapped and bordered by our imaginations. Words are among the markers that our imaginations set out to do this defining work. In the Christian imagination, words are of great importance. Words spoken in and about certain places—by certain people—help define a place we love. The Word of God is a layered theological concept. The words of people we love—remembered, retold, perhaps even altered and edited throughout our lives—surround our vocations, families, and residences with history, context, and meaning. In the Gospel of John, the story of life begins in the womb-like darkness:

> In the beginning was the Word, and the Word was with God, and the Word was God. He was in the beginning with God. All things came into being through him, and without him not one thing came into being. What has come into being in him was life, and the life was the light of all people. The light shines in the darkness, and the darkness has not overcome it. (John 1:1–5)

A *Word* is at the beginning of all things: creative potential, luminous life.

In Luke's Gospel, Gabriel's words about the baby Mary will bear define places; he makes reference to territories of earth and an extensive kingdom:

> He will be great, and will be called the Son of the Most High, and the Lord God will give to him the throne of his ancestor David. He will reign over the house

of Jacob forever, and of his kingdom there will be no
end. (Luke 1:32–33)

With the announcement of a birth, the first chapter of a book
of life opens. The light in the womb becomes the light of the
world. In John, "The Word became flesh and lived among
us, . . . full of grace and truth" (John 1:14). In Luke's Gospel,
words specify a certain place, establish a unique birth event,
and create a web of memory:

> While they were there, the time came for her to de-
> liver her child. And she gave birth to her firstborn son
> and wrapped him in bands of cloth, and laid him in
> a manger, because there was no place for them in the
> inn. (Luke 2:6–7)

Mary's Place

Art historian Jeremy Wood writes that from about the second
half of the thirteenth century "the Nativity began to be shown
in increasingly human terms." Mary, the mother, occupied the
central place, of course, with Joseph nearby or in the shad-
ows. Showing relationships and interactions between Mary,
Joseph, shepherds, wise men, and others is an artistic innova-
tion of this period. This chapter explores the ways in which
parents (and those who stand in for parents) create beloved
places, especially through their children.

A quick survey of Christmas hymns in the *Lutheran Book
of Worship* reveals that for every hymn that bends down and
directs words to or about the baby Jesus or Mary, there are ten
that treat the theology of the Christmas story, the emotions of

those who have heard the story, or some other broader concern around the narration of the birth of Jesus. In comparison, five of the nine Christmas hymns included in a recently published African American hymnal comment on the baby or Mary.[2] The editors of that hymnal, like some of our best poets, know that the story of the nativity begins with Mary; in telling and retelling the story they stay close to her.

Mother and Child

With the announcement of Mary's pregnancy in Luke, lines of prophecy are exposed and the essential line of action and meaning turns around Mary, because the baby is in her and then, in birth, near her. A poem written in the 1970s by the writer and farmer Wendell Berry, titled "Manifesto: The Mad Farmer Liberation Front," is a stream of contrarian, agricultural, value-laden comment and advice. A few lines from the middle of it apply to this discussion:

> So long as women do not go cheap
> for power, please women more than men.
> Ask yourself: Will this satisfy
> a woman satisfied to bear a child?
> Will this disturb the sleep
> of a woman near to giving birth?[3]

It is common to view the birth of a child as a hopeful event. Adults predict and foresee achievements and a promising future in the tiny body of the infant they love. Surely this little one will occupy the White House, play Carnegie Hall, or compete on the PGA tour. This small bundle will grow up to fame and fortune and draw all who love her to comfort and happiness. Christians magnify this kind of hope in the baby Jesus. The family is a multitude, the loved ones are waves of generations around the world:

> From heaven above to earth I come
> To bring good news to everyone!
> Glad tidings of great joy I bring
> To all the world and gladly sing.[4]

The imagination creates works of art and other objects and projects by envisioning, forming, shaping, ordering, and so on. The imagination may also be an instrument of love, an outpouring of the self in a creative act in response to an observation, to a set of circumstances, to one's surroundings. Many Christians believe that creation was and continues to be an act of divine love. Loving attention followed by disciplined action in relation to the object of that attention may result in a creation of something new. This theological principle of renewal and redemption is found throughout the Christian scripture.

In Mark's Gospel, Jesus returns to the territory of his ministry after a period in the wilderness and announces, "The kingdom of God has come near" (Mark 1:15). The landscape looks the same, but the intentions of this one resident are now heard, and through the deeds of his life others would see their ordinary places in new ways. In Paul's letter to the Ephesians we read a building plan based on "the mystery of gospel." People are renewed in their outlooks and their identities. Then attachment to a place renews that place through the eyes of faith and love. The beloved place is constructed "on the foundation of the apostles and prophets" with "Christ Jesus himself as the cornerstone" (Ephesians 2:20). This is a spiritual building in a corner of an invisible kingdom, but those who constitute it might re-imagine the concrete world they live in through the influence of their citizenship in this fellowship of faith.

Christians love the world because through the eyes of faith they see it as a creation and as a gift. As a response to a work of art exhibited in a gallery might be appreciation or criticism, the Christian response to the created world might be praise and stewardship. These responses serve to identify the faithful person with the world. Through faith in Christ they are themselves renewed as a "place": "If any one is in Christ, there is a new creation" (2 Corinthians 5:17). Faith intuits this spiritual arrangement. What Paul calls the "mystery of the gospel" (Ephesians 6:19) feeds this understanding of life.

As one can say that the imagination grasps a story told, conversely one might say that the story has grabbed the imagination. This circular apprehension (holding and being held, understanding and being understood, for example) seems fundamental to Christian teaching and is a principle that may illuminate the human love of place. A living reciprocity obtains: the place holds us; then we hold the place in our hearts and our memories. We imagine an ideal place; then we try to create it. A dynamic partnership between people and place such as between the field and the farmer, the farmer and the field, respects the power and influence of both partners. Winston Churchill once said in reference to architecture, "First we shape the building, then the building shapes us."

Human attention to a certain location may create a place

of memory and emotional attachment. As the imagination "holds" a place, frames and defines it, the place holds the person. The places we love are the places that we and others before us have imagined and created. The few paragraphs of the biblical infancy narrative are for many people a "place" that the imagination has created and recreated. The imagined Bethlehem and the sequence of events that lead to it and from it comprise what most people think of as the Christmas story and trigger memories and thoughts of other beloved places: childhood churches, family gatherings, holiday cheer, disappointments and pains. As we read back and forth between the biblical scene of Jesus' birth on one hand, and the places and scenes of our own lives on the other hand, we may test and strengthen our love for each one.

Announcing Birth

The birth is the beginning and the first essential piece of information. A baby is born. A birthplace is established and loved to some degree if only for the import of that singular event. Parents know how the birth of a child changes their lives forever. In our world, the wise men and women who attend the mother and baby at the moment of birth are doctors, nurses, and medical technicians.

The renowned American poet William Carlos Williams (1883–1963) practiced medicine for many years in and around Paterson, New Jersey. By the time he retired from the position of co-director of pediatrics at Passaic General Hospital, he had delivered three thousand babies. Through the years of his medical practice during the first half of the twentieth century, Dr. Williams simultaneously practiced untraditional composition of poetry in the American vernacular. In his poem "The Gift" he turned to the infancy narrative in the gospels from the perspective of a witness to the birth of a human baby, and to the activities immediately following the birth. Williams's instincts as a physician and his imagination as a poet agree with the African American Christmas hymns: the central and crucial components of the story are the baby and the mother. Variations on the simple, essential facts of life-begun-in-birth were the repeating rounds of a single story Williams knew well.

> . . . the imagination
>   knows all stories
>   before they are told
> and knows the truth of this one
>   past all defection.[5]

The poem begins with the bemused observation that gold ornaments, frankincense, and myrrh were brought to the "birthplace / of the god of love" by old, genuflecting "wise men" in priestly robes:

> The rich gifts
>   so unsuitable for a child
>   though devoutly proffered,
> stood for all that love can bring.
>   The men were old
>   how could they know
> of a mother's needs
>   or a child's
>   appetite?

Reflected in these extravagantly inappropriate gifts is the gift of life itself. Williams's nativity image draws upon a tradition from the visual arts; as the wise men delivered their gifts of recognition and praise,

> the devils
>> as an old print shows
> retreated in confusion.

When new life appears as a gift of love and is met with praise in the return of love, devils flee the scene. They cannot occupy this place. Like the outlaw cowboys of a Western song who are punished after death by an eternity of chasing "the devil's herd across the endless sky,"[6] the devils' nature is to flee from the moments of love-come-to-life in birth. The devils, along with their attendants, the cursed and the damned of the world, have no sabbath rest, no sanctuary, no point of origin, and no destination. The mutual transaction of love offered, love received, and love returned poisons the place for them. In their retreat from the birth and its aftermath, they fulfill their own destiny and give their own kind of praise according to their nature. Praise, the spontaneous outpouring of life, creates a place that the mind remembers and to which the heart returns. The devils define the place by their departure. The wise men, with praise in their hands, define the place by their presence and their attentions of love.

> But as they kneeled
>> the child was fed.
>> They saw it
> and gave praise!

A Holy Place

A holy place is one set apart from the ordinary. All places we know, remember, long for, and love are set apart and are therefore in some sense holy. As the wise men knelt they confirmed that this mythical manger of birth was a "place" to which human imaginations could return. Through countless returns of generations of people to this manger, the place would be further defined, its holiness refined in bending, attention, and praise.

So, in summary, a preliminary point suggested by this poem is that praise—the extravagant outpouring of love—defines "place." The birth of "the god of love"—complete with ridiculous gifts proffered, reverent guests, the poet's imaginative attention, inspired in part by a painter's imagination, which in turn had been inspired by the Bible—all of these overlapping and interlocking acts of love and praise define a "place" to which the imagination may return.

"Place" belongs to the defining imagination and to the heart's overflowing of praise, innocently and even ignorantly attending to a mystery. The poet defines "place" in the mystery of his or her creative imagination. "[T]he imagination / knows all stories / before they are told," wrote Williams. The imagination is an instrument of praise, and praise is an instrument of creation with the power to form places we love out of spaces we inhabit. Praise may be verbal joy in the presence of a loved one. The worshipers offer songs of praise. The mother and father offer praise of the child, sometimes in syllables resembling parental glossolalia.

Praise, Poetry, and Place

From the moment of birth, words surround the baby. Parents speak intimate nonsense near a baby's head. They repeat the child's name with drawn-out vowels, their lips rounded and their mouths full of air. They make sounds of nesting birds. They hum and sing. Nonsense syllables and songs surround the baby in auditory comfort and security. Parents and grandparents cluck and coo. The human voice makes a place for the baby and the parent together. The place the baby loves is the place where the mother's voice is heard. This should go without saying. The mother's low assurances of her presence are basic poetry to the baby: these words cannot be paraphrased. Their powerful effect lies in something other than translatable meaning. Sound and sense, order and meaning, may be tossed and jumbled in the immediate, intimate refrains of love from a mother's mouth to her baby's ear. The words of a mother to the baby in her arms are the first definition of a place we love. The words of a parent to an infant constitute the first and primary poetry of our love of place. As children grow, the places they love continue to be defined by their parents' voices.

As a little boy grows, he needs to hear his father's voice change into the sound of a rumbling bear or a huffing bull. A delight of family travel might be the hearing of familiar "home" voices in an unfamiliar place. The effect of traveling companions on us—especially of parents on children—may be to quickly "stake out" a place we love by the juxtaposition of voices we know, heard in a new environment. Familiar and even visceral sounds that convey emotions—rage, delight, pride—are heard all through life. In "Waving Goodbye," a poem by Gerald Stern, communication between a parent and

a grown child still reaches down into that primal region of
syllables, growls, and sighs too deep for words:

> . . . I drove my daughter through the snow to meet
> her friend
> and filled her car with suitcases and hugged her
> as an animal would, pressing my forehead against her,
> walking in circles, moaning, touching her cheek . . .[7]

Even without words, the love of a father for his grown child is
still heard in a diffused form of sound.

A Book of Life

If you asked me today to name my favorite book, I would
show you a certain poetry anthology. I bought my copy, many
years ago, in a used bookshop. I enjoy the book's cover as well
as its shape, its size, and what I imagine of its past, as much
as I enjoy the literary content of its pages. A personal note,
loose inside the cover—typed by and to people unknown to
me—has survived there nearly half a century. To me the note
and the book stand for the benefit of memory, the power of
language, and the surprising and salutary connections made
through reading—especially reading aloud across generations
and through the years.

Poems such as the ones contained in that anthology offer
visual patterns of measured lines constructed of words chosen
for meaning and sound, alone and in relation to other words.
Syntax, rhythm, rhyme—the qualities of poetry—do not seem
to be matters of immediate value. The important and news-
worthy enterprises—the accidents and rescues of our lives

and times—are reported, cheered, and opined publicly and regularly. Poems, artifacts made of words, do not deliver the latest national news, celebrity gossip, or stock market tips, but they might be small performance packages that can shape our minds and hearts to more humane and satisfying—if not more Godly—perspectives on our mortal days.

"Teach us to count our days," wrote the Psalmist, "that we may gain a wise heart" (90:12). Some poems may present exercises in counting. Careful readers might say, following the Psalmist, *Teach us to count syllables and accents.* . . . Patterns of syllable beats, connected in lines, are divisions of time. Rhythm and rhyme, the interrelated patterns of movement and sound, combine with meaning and sense, reference and tone, in the complex artistic package of a poem. Similarly, every human life can be measured as a created, living poem, in rhythms of time and lines of years, with objective meaning and emotional intensity contained in various units of historical record and emotional color.

The Place of Words

The reading aloud of a poem—a creation in words punctuated out of primeval respect for the breath of our lungs, the pumping of the blood from our hearts, the evolution of our eyesight for words on a page—may be an exercise in marking and measuring time. Reading a poem aloud may be a small performance of some of the forces that divide and frame time and meaning, sound and sense. Poems, especially lyric poems, are compact compositions with a beginning and an end just like each human life, and, like human lives, not all of them run along in smooth lines with pleasing and predictable resolutions. Reading good poems requires allowance for ambiguity and open-ended, unresolved segments of thought and sound. Abrupt enjambments may end a line of a poem—or a year of life or a job or a relationship—suddenly and without warning. I have lost track of my favorite book's origination in the stream of my life. I count this mystery of its origin as one of the book's virtues. I have searched my memory, stared hard at it, and still have been unable to recall specifically where I bought it. I can say with a high degree of certainty that I must have bought it for a good price one day in the fall or spring in the early or mid-eighties, at a used bookstore in Chatham or in a converted barn in the Connecticut countryside north or west of New Haven. Less likely, but perhaps, I bought it in one of those musty shops in Cambridge or Boston that smell faintly of paper mold and cause my wife to sneeze and somehow remind me of Christmas. I cannot recall where or exactly when it became mine, so the book carries an added air of being given to me, delivered by some patron or angel while I slept.

As I hold the book in my hands today I like the weight and the size of it, as I must have liked it on the now-forgotten day that I bought it. At nearly three hundred fifty heavy pages it asserts itself among the slimmer paperbacks on my shelf. It has no dust jacket. The color of the cardboard cover is close to that of our family's old army surplus tent. Thin black and gray slack-string striping hangs like stretched-then-slackened string through the green. The book's binding is mustard yellow with the black and gray string-stripe running, less pleasingly, horizontally. The title and author are printed in black on a block of the green:

Poems to Read Aloud
Hodnett

This anthology of poetry, selected and edited by Edward Hodnett, was published in 1957.

A Place in History

Nineteen fifty-seven. Eisenhower was in the White House. Sputnik was in orbit. *Leave It to Beaver* was on the air. Enamored of television, Americans were becoming a nation of voyeurs, squeezing together into corners of our living rooms to watch the glowing screen. Possessed by suspicion of the Russians, we were becoming a nation of paranoids, ready to squeeze into underground bunkers at a moment's notice. In 1957 we were losing sight of life-as-we-knew-it. The advance of technology and the human proclivity to violence was eroding our sense of ourselves as secure, prosperous, and happy people. The vast blackness of space threatened, and the black of a television screen that followed our favorite programs was making us anxious. We needed then, as we need now—in the face of new technologies and new perceived threats—new minds and hearts to re-imagine ourselves and our lives together. Communities constituted by and for the power of words helped then, as they help today.

The composition of Hodnett's anthology gives one a sense of a literary communion of saints, dead and alive, living on through families and in community through their created words. The contents are arranged alphabetically by the poets' surnames. Other anthologies I own are assembled in other ways. One is put together according to poetic categories of voice, language, dramatic structure, and so on, by a recognized authority in the field. One is organized according to theme. The rest of the anthologies on my shelf are of the all-star type, organized historically, with early English poets coming first in full representation and a few contemporary poet honorees ushered in at the end. The chronological arrangement follows a scholar's management of the field and falls in line with the presumptions of academic dissertations, critical comparisons, and analyses. Some recent anthologies are marketed with emphasis on the editor's well-known name. A twist of creative writing from Robert Pinsky blesses each section of one recently published volume. Satirist Garrison Keillor's homely *imprimatur* adorns another.

The otherwise uncategorized alphabetical order of Hodnett's *Poems to Read Aloud* makes the volume seem like a community directory, similar to the directory of families in my sons' elementary school or to our church membership booklet—a directory with many entries that are familiar. The list begins with "Aiken, Conrad, 1889—" and continues with names of many poets whose work and voices are called to mind by their mere mention:

Anonymous
Arnold, Matthew 1822–1888
Auden, W. H. 1907–
Benet, Stephen Vincent 1889–1943
Blake, William 1757–1827

The gathered community of wordsmiths runs through to an anticipated luminous end:

Wilbur, Richard 1921–
Wilde, Oscar 1856–1900
Wolfe, Charles 1792–1823
Wordsworth, William 1770–1850
Wyatt, Sir Thomas 1503?–1542
Wylie, Elinor 1885–1928
Yeats, William Butler 1865–1939

With this directory in hand one can, on an evening in mid-winter, turn to Thomas Campion 1567–1620, for example, and hear his poem "Now Winter Nights Enlarge," a few lines of which read:

> Let now the chimneys blaze,
> And cups o'erflow with wine;
> Let well-tuned words amaze
> With harmony divine.

Well-tuned words amaze from within, the way wine amazes the body from within on the longest nights of the year. Well-tuned words blend one century's concerns with another's in cultural harmonics, sonically repairing the time-weathered and violence-damaged walls of the human imagination.

Hodnett introduces his choices of read-aloud poems by stating his criteria for inclusion: a wide range of poems to appeal to "the taste of all sorts of readers, moods and occasions."[8] He must have had in mind that these poems should be enjoyed with the eye and then, for a fuller experience, in the mouth: spoken and tasted. Hodnett hoped that the readers of this book would speak these poems out loud, claiming, by way of his introduction, that reading aloud provides a pleasure of speaking and hearing and, furthermore, that *reading aloud is the best way to understand the meaning of a poem. Listening to it being read is the next best.* His introduction includes helpful advice about finding one's way into a satisfying experience of reading aloud, especially in groups.

I trust that such groups coalesced at his suggestion in the late fifties, and that some exist today, even beyond the degree-required reading groups of MFA programs around the country. Though I am in favor of such focused human cooperation and literary fellowship, I have never been part of a reading group. I have, however, read some of the poems of this book aloud to groups captive to, if not always captivated by, the sound of my reading voice: to my boys in their bedrooms (for example, "Bears" by Arthur Guiterman 1871–1943 and "The Seal's Lullaby" by Rudyard Kipling 1865–1936 after our vacation in Alaska) and to my congregation on Sunday mornings. Failing the formation of reading groups, the poems carry their sound into the world anyway.

When Hodnett writes in favor of reading aloud, he *means* reading *aloud*; but good poems, created as they are of verbal packages, cannot help but carry sound. In the back of the head—near the place where the spoken word reverberates its signals—a poem read even silently is always *heard.* There should be little controversy about Hodnett's assertions that many poems are best heard in social interaction, and that the best forum for a poem is an audible one. This is true in part because what is contained in a poem, and discovered there by readers and listeners, should be discussed and shared. Nevertheless, discoveries made in the reading of poems may also be tucked away, kept and pondered, as Mary kept the memory and descriptions of the events around her.

An Eternal Place

The word creates life from the earth. A poem is a creation of words, a verbal sculpture worked up out of the elements of life. The words of a poem, if they are attuned to the earth, are a receivable stream of observation and an object of art sent and created from the senses of a single human being for reception by the senses of others. This gift is not a hot potato or a fading flower. Good things last. Good books maintain their value through the years and generations. A good gift of words, even one given long ago, may help us count our days by reminding us of the contingencies, connections, and limits of life. Old books—especially those created and first enjoyed before our time—may draw us into cultural and personal contemplations that will help us "stand firm and hold fast to the traditions that [we] were taught . . . by word of mouth or by letter" (2 Thessalonians 2:15).

The Heart's Place

Mary, pondering what she had seen and heard, did not turn words into stories or assertions and peddle them down the road of Christian devotion. She kept these things she had received— even the great poetic gift of God—in the heart's eternal place and in her memory. The heart has its own playback system, its own vibrations through the air of intellect. A poem read aloud once may be heard again and again in silent remembrance, meditation, and study. As long as there are gifted poets writing, editors like Hodnett assembling poems with humility and care, and people reading and giving books as gifts for others to read, the words will be heard through the years, decade after decade. Hodnett's recommendations about a method for reading may be profitably received: A reader might begin by trying to catch the tone of a poem, then move on to determining how the thought develops in it, then to discerning the rhythm, and so on. Finally a poem should be tasted by speaking it aloud. I would add that it might be most profitably read aloud in the presence of another interested person. If the other is a person of another generation, all the better.

The Psalmist wrote, "taste and see that the LORD is good" (34:8). The word of God is not the word *to us* unless it is spoken and heard *by us.* Paul wrote that faith comes by hearing (see Romans 10:17). Words live in the context of a language. Language is our medium of communication and cultural transmission, and it is a workhorse. Words loaded with threats of violence or with promises of reconciliation carry us outside ourselves. Words are weapons and olive branches, new creations reflecting current culture and artifacts carrying the living soil and dying dust of other centuries. Sculpted, lyric word creations have their own nearly sacramental standing. They are made to be tasted in a sensate order: writing, reading, speaking, and hearing. The word is our word when it is at our fingers, before our eyes, on our lips, in our ears. John's Gospel begins with the declaration that the word became flesh. The words we have been given, and the words we have created ourselves, become flesh when they are told, tasted, and known again.

My copy of the Hodnett anthology once belonged to other people who are unknown to me except for the note that was left inside the front cover. Somewhere in the uneasy America of 1957 an unnamed mother bought this book of poems. She must have chosen it from the shelf, handed it to a clerk, and paid for it. I imagine that before she wrapped it in gift paper and brown mailing paper to send, I surmise, to her son or daughter and his or her spouse, she composed a note to them, neatly typed it, and placed it inside the front cover.

The top edge of the half-sheet of typing paper, folded like a card, today is torn slightly and discolored. Three of the surfaces are blank. On the facing page are these words, typed just like this:

If you read what this man says, you
will come across: "In these days of
millions of Americans who spend millions of hours in cars, movies and before
television sets, it is no minor triumph
to prove that you're alive. Reading
poetry keeps you alert and to a lesser
degree, listening to it does, too.
Poets are peculiarly equipped to give you
insights into the profound aspects of
human experience. . . . . . Reading poetry
aloud will in time improve your own
writing and speaking. . . . they are models
of economy, exactness and grace of
expression."

Since you are both models of most
everything in most everything and
since neither of you spends many hours

in cars, movies or before television,
you will probably exclaim, "Then <u>why</u>
did the old girl <u>send</u> us this!"

Well . . . I just thought it was full of
lovely things to read—aloud or otherwise.
　　　　　　Mom.

The note—like the poems of the book and like the book itself—wraps good things in words and gives them away as signs of love, without superfluous salutations asserting what is already carried in the words themselves.

Copying these lines I imagine this mom at her typewriter, her right hand reaching to grasp and pull the return lever at the end of each short line, a motion unnecessary in the line-without-end of our word-processing programs. Retracing her typing on my computer keyboard I try to retrace her thoughts: unsentimental, risking the embarrassment of cultural pretension and emotional excess to offer a gift of good things to her children. As I imagine her, I think of my own mother, a reader whose letters have a permanent place in my memory.

When this mom wrote the note to her kids she had likely read the first poem of the anthology, or at least noticed its title: "All Lovely Things" by Conrad Aiken 1889–. The poem is a lyric lament about *the loss* of lovely things. Youth and love, like the flowers of spring, pass into autumn and then pass away. The poem begins:

All lovely things will have an ending,
All lovely things will fade and die, . . .

Thoughts like these might sink us, threaten to drown us in depression if we did not have mothers to love us and children to inspire us. The first line of the second stanza reads: "Fine ladies all are soon forgotten." The love of a mother, however, even of unknown mothers, is not forgotten.

The taste and living energy of our language are not forgotten either, because our words are full of life that may be tasted and heard in speech and sound, and renewed in giving and receiving. Words, the fundamental building blocks of our lives and spirits, may reform us into people who cherish the past even as we care for, love, and create the world around us with the coming generation in mind. The reading aloud of works of art made of words may help us learn to weigh and measure the value and span of our days on earth.

Master, now you are dismissing your
servant in peace
according to your word;
for my eyes have seen your salvation,
which you have prepared in the
presence of all peoples,
a light for revelation to the Gentiles
and for glory to your people Israel.

LUKE 2:29–32

Jerusalem, my happy home,
Would God I were in thee!
Would God my woes were at an end,
Thy joys that I might see!

A SIXTEENTH-CENTURY HYMN

So part we sadly in this troublous world,
To meet with joy in sweet Jerusalem.

WILLIAM SHAKESPEARE, *HENRY VI*, PART 3, V.V

Five

JERUSALEM

THE STORY OF JESUS' LIFE, in Matthew's account, moves quickly out of the "little town" of Bethlehem and onto roads of exile into Egypt. Luke's version of the story tells how Mary and Joseph kept the Law of Moses and went up to Jerusalem to fulfill the covenant-naming tradition. The story of Jesus then runs out on roads and villages around the Sea of Galilee, and then, following the flow of the Jordan, down to the Holy City of Jerusalem again, the capital of God's people. The story of Jesus, and of God's people who preceded Jesus as well as those who follow him, cannot resist the gravitational attraction of the city. The story of Jesus does not end as it began, on a silent night in a small town. It ends violently, in the city but outside the gates that mark off privilege and power. The final ritual of sacrifice and of naming, corresponding to the ritual of sacrifice and naming at the beginning of Jesus' life, takes place in the city. The final beloved place—where love of God and love of neighbor are exercised fully—is the city.

This chapter orbits Jerusalem, the city of God on earth and the emblem of Christian hope. These two beloved Jerusalems share borders in the Christian universe. The first is situated over layered history several millennia deep, on the ridge at the edge of the Judean Desert, sixty miles east of the Mediterranean and twenty miles west of the Dead Sea. The other is the New Jerusalem of Christian ritual return and eschatological hope, mapped in scripture and located in faithful hearts. Jerusalem is the home of God's people, the city of King David and of Jesus, in David's line. Jerusalem has been and is the site of internecine bloodshed and of cultic and devotional pilgrimage. The two Jerusalems are not identical but they are inseparable. The sacramental vision, evanesced through time and sacred ways, is not blotted out by a ravaged history. Centuries of power plays, infused more with politics than with prayer, have again and again ground and pounded Jerusalem, mixing its dust with blood. But the "city" still shines on its holy hill. Its walls surround worshiping communities all over the world.

Jerusalem, as the Christian symbol of hope and return, is a bud stemming from the vine of ancient Israel. The city that Christians hold dear is the very heart of Jewish identity and devotion. Elie Wiesel's writings evoke Jerusalem in stirrings that reach outward, widely and generally, and inward, particularly and painfully. When Wiesel was a little boy, Jerusalem was the fantasy stage, the enveloping dream, of his young life:

> A melodious name, evocative of a distant, familiar
> yet unknown past, a name that soothed even as it
> inspired awe, especially with advent of night, at the
> twilight hour when children are afraid to stay alone.
> Someone would hum a lullaby or teach me a prayer.

I would close my eyes and discover a spellbound and spellbinding city taking form in a dream. . . . I knew it was Jerusalem. . . . The child in me loved it more than he loved his native town. I belonged to it, I roamed its alleys, I lost myself in its shadow. And my own mood reflected its successive glories and desolation.[1]

One dark night he and many others traveled there. It was a dream city still, a nightmare city:

Barbed wire, everywhere barbed wire, and above us, a sky in flames. Surrounding me were travel companions who like myself were staring, hoping for a sign, a clue. Was there a key to this nightmare? The moaning prisoners, the officers shouting their commands, the barking dogs, the demented cries heard from afar: sounds and sights that evoked no memory, no echo. . . . Men and women and children torn from every land, bearers of every name in Jewish history, representing every facet of destiny—I saw them converge on this place, this exalted place of mankind in the shadow of stakes from another era. And suddenly a shattering thought crossed my mind: this is Jerusalem, this is the hour of redemption. . . . Jerusalem, both earthly and heavenly, opening its doors to its inhabitants, dead and living, come to glorify her at midnight.[2]

This is Jerusalem: the city of bloody horror and the city of salvation. For Christians, the setting of an ordinary story of defeat in shameful death turns into the narration of final victory in Jerusalem. This night-and-day Jerusalem, this dualism, is a fundamental premise of this chapter: the city of hope crumbles again and again under the weight of human activity, yet human beings keep bolstering the walls of Jerusalem, rebuilding her gates, crying for blessing in the dust of her alleyways, turning human political attention there, pinning whatever hope remains on earth to the legends of her streets. The Jerusalem described here is a multifaceted ideal and a brutally complex real place, a beloved heavenly city and beloved place on earth.

Territorial claims to the earthly Jerusalem are made on the basis of might, tenure, privilege, and custodial care. Christians, Muslims, and Jews return to Jerusalem every day as if they are returning to their own cities. By the eighth century, Muslim commentators agreed that Prophet Muhammad's momentous night journey was to the "distant" shrine in Jerusalem, sacred city of Abraham, Moses, and Jesus, thereby mapping an Islamic mystical and passionate lifeline there. In this book we follow Christian routes to Jerusalem, on roads of local liturgy and devotional pilgrimage. These ways are crowded and shared; the religious meaning of the city is densely packed. The lines of ownership, of blood rights and tradition, of military power and political influence, crowd—indeed, one might say, have created—the story of Jerusalem. Christians return to Jerusalem on particular, but not exclusive, ways.

To Christians, Jerusalem is the heart's home because it is the soil of decisive and formative New Testament events and therefore the locus of sacramental return in the Lord's Supper. It is the locus, too, of faithful devotional and doctrinal reading of scripture. Jerusalem is the final symbol of hope, incarnate in a diverse community of human beings, in the often God-forsaken, human-made environment of the city.

Three points form the frame and flesh of these reflections on Jerusalem as the city we love:

1. Jerusalem is the spiritual and ritual *home* in the liturgy of the Holy Communion.
2. Jerusalem has been and continues to be the destination and beloved place of pilgrims who come "home" to the troubled place, which they may have never been to before but which they have "seen" countless times.
3. Jerusalem is the city of God and therefore home to God's people in a broad, final view.

These three facets of Jerusalem—the sacramental center of ritual return, the holy place of pilgrimage, and the eschatological city of God—are interrelated in the Christian universe. The connections weave through and wrap down and around the actual streets of the Old City, into the pathways of a heart informed by doctrine learned and grace received. A powerful, supple Christian faith might hold the symbol and the city together, as they might be held together in the singing of the sixteenth-century ballad quoted above: "Jerusalem, my happy home, / would God I were in thee!"

Jerusalem as Home in Liturgy

Christians can hardly consider Jerusalem, the city or the symbol, without trading on the biblical vision of the new Jerusalem recorded in the Book of Revelation. The passage is one of the propers in the service for Burial of the Dead. It limns the eschatological dimension of the city and therein its indelible holy mien and continuing religious meaning for Christians:

> And I saw the Holy City, the new Jerusalem, coming down out of heaven from God, prepared as a bride adorned for her husband. And I heard a loud voice from the throne saying,
> "See, the home of God is among mortals.
> He will dwell with them;
> they will be his peoples,
> and God himself will be with them;
> he will wipe every tear from their eyes.
> Death will be no more;
> mourning and crying and pain will be no more,
> for the first things have passed away."
> (Revelation 21: 2–4)

This is the Jerusalem that veils and completes all the city's famous risings and crumblings, the Jerusalem that summarizes every Sunday school career and every long life of weekly liturgical participation. The Jerusalem of Revelation is one of the central halls in the corporate memory mansion of Christians. Here in Jerusalem is the border country of death, the gate of life. Here, wherever the congregation gathers for Christian worship, is Jerusalem.

The Place of Worship

Jonathan Z. Smith advances the argument that the new Jerusalem, independent of place, is condensed for Christians in the liturgical year as it is condensed for Jews in Mishnah.[3] He writes that

the theory of place involves a focus on the individual
and his or her subjective experience, which trans-
forms "place" to "home." One's place of birth may be
accidental; but investing it with meaning, converting
it into a home, is an act of human construction. This
transformative act becomes a paradigm of all humane
activity: the conversion of mere location into a locus
of significance. To have a home is to have built.[4]

Smith refers to the "technology" of ritual,[5] meaning that
ritual, of which the liturgy is an example, is an application
of knowledge. In the liturgy the assembly applies its received
knowledge to a social activity, a complex ritual, which, the
assembly believes, returns it to a source of power. The knowledge is a Word, the divine *Logos*. The power received through
the social ritual action is described theologically and inter-
nally (within the city) as forgiveness of sin, eternal life, salvation, and so on. Isolated individuals do not receive this power;
in the gathering of individuals, doing their prescribed work
in the Holy Communion, it is received. In other words, the
power is received in the city, the place that the people of God
have built together, through division of duties and over generations, and to which they make their ritual returns. This city
is a place of power and of danger, of blessing and of opportu-
nity, in which people are at home with God.

The liturgy is, literally and in reality, the work of the people.
When the community gathers to sing and listen, to pray and
proclaim, to wash hands and share bread and wine, its members do their proper, prescribed work. As they repeat these
actions they make a holy home for themselves in the world. To
have a home with God is to have worked with God according
to the plan of the liturgy. Just as the temple was built according

to a divine plan, given by David to Solomon,[6] the liturgy is a given (and already accomplished) work.

According to Smith, people obtain a sense of place through the creation of "mental maps."[7] When the familiar maps are followed, they direct a people home. The movement in the liturgy, to the center and to the holy things, is conveyed by speaking over and over the "plan" of the liturgy as a map. God gives it in substance in the words of scripture and, in structure, in tradition. Smith writes:

> In contrast to the modern focus on individual perception, we must keep in mind . . . [that] place is not created, it is given. Human beings seek their place, conform to their place, fulfill their place. They do so by keeping their place. From the classical point of view, place is neither individual nor egalitarian. Place is preeminently social and hierarchical.[8]

When Christians gather on Sunday morning they begin their roadwork. They come home to the new Jerusalem. They follow a given way, a pattern of service, a map that draws them in and recreates for them, the city of Jerusalem. As they do the work of the liturgy God works through them, drawing them to himself in the spiritual Jerusalem. There is a clear hierarchy of order, around which the assembly works and moves: word and sacrament, reading and meal, spirit and body, voice and presence.

In the *Kyrie* the people begin the last steps of their pilgrimage from the distant corners of secular life, from the foreign territories of their work and leisure. For a week, more or less, they have been in exile in a hostile world: "If you invoke as

Father the one who judges all people impartially according to their deeds, live in reverent fear during the time of your exile" (1 Peter 1:17). Their worship is a weekly furlough. They are gathered in reunion. In Hebrews we read that the life of faith is a pilgrimage to a city undertaken by people who have

> confessed that they were strangers and foreigners on the earth, for people who speak in this way make it clear that they are seeking a homeland. If they had been thinking of the land that they had left behind, they would have had opportunity to return. But as it is, they desire a better country, that is, a heavenly one. Therefore God is not ashamed to be called their God; indeed, he has prepared a city for them. (Hebrews 11:13–16)

At the hymn of praise, having come close to God by virtue of their assembly with others, they shout for joy. Then, having heard the word of God, they confess their faith in the pattern of ancient words. They pray and make their offerings. As the gifts of their hands and the gifts for the meal are brought forward, an offertory is sung, one of which asks, and quickly answers:

> What shall I render to the Lord for all his benefits to me? I will offer the sacrifice of thanksgiving and will call on the name of the Lord. I will take the cup of salvation and will call on the name of the Lord. I will pay my vows to the Lord now in the presence of all his people, in the courts of the Lord's house, in the midst of you, O Jerusalem.[9]

At the Great Thanksgiving the people have arrived in Jerusalem and are seated, "on the night in which he was betrayed," for the meal. The journey, the pilgrimage of the people, is complete in the spiritual Jerusalem, given by God in Christ, constructed by the servant people in a ritual work. The sacramental space given by God in Christ is rebuilt again and again in the Holy Communion. In this newly built city of Jerusalem, God's people are at home around the table. They are fed with the bread and wine of the Holy Communion, the body and blood of Christ. The Old Testament scholar Robert Wilson writes that

> In contrast to the commonly held opinion that the Israelites were relative latecomers to cities, Israel's own accounts of its origins place the creation of cities at the very beginning of human life on earth. . . . It was in the city that life as the historian knew it—as we know it—began to grow.[10]

The city is the place where things happen, where human creativity flowers and commerce is conducted. In the city, ritually built by the repeated liturgy of the church, life is given by God.

Jerusalem as the Pilgrim's Home

To people immersed in the ritual world described above, to those who are in the habit of returning to Jerusalem every week and to building it together according to the divine plan of the liturgy, the historical, temporal Jerusalem is attractive as a spiritual center on earth. In the incarnational faith of the church, the divine Word became flesh, God came to dwell with us, the king was enthroned in Jerusalem—in the Temple and on the Cross. This complex and fundamental creative spiritual tension lies near the heart of the Christian tradition, claiming that the divine has entered human form. The Jerusalem of history has drawn believers, especially since Constantine (AD 306–337), to a ritual return, to pilgrimage through time and space, to a city built of stone for the benefit of one's spirit.

Christians must pause here. Pilgrimage has not always been an innocent and blameless return to the source of life. A spiritualized view cannot cover the dark madness of the human heart that turns a beloved place into a place of demonic attraction. A pilgrim band may be an invading army in disguise. The Crusades are an obvious historical example.

Around the year AD 1000, Christian pilgrims began to stream from Western Europe to the city of Jerusalem. There, cultures—East and West, Christianity and Islam, indeed, civilizations of Europe and Asia—collided in a bloody religious and cultural rage that would transfigure the world in ways that reverberate to this day. The details of the Crusades are beyond the range of this book. It is sufficient to hear this reminder that in those days the streets of Jerusalem ran deep with the blood of innocents. As the Christian liturgy begins in confession, travel pilgrimage might begin the same way, blessing the suffering of innocents long past, remembering the human darkness that reigns regularly on the streets of Jerusalem. So burdened is the ancient city by the highest human expectations that it crumbles repeatedly under that weight. Suffering and death follow. Yet Jerusalem calls pilgrims to return, to grieve in her streets, and to rebuild the city.

A pilgrimage is a journey home to a place where one has likely never been. The Christian pilgrim in Jerusalem, accustomed to worshiping according to a liturgical map, will have built the city many times and will feel at home in it. The pilgrim who accomplishes the journey home will see with eyes informed by mental maps of his spiritual home. He will let the smells and sights of the place adorn and complete the map he carries inside of himself. Walking the ancient and modern ways of Jerusalem can unite a pilgrim with a wider congregation the world over as well as with those who have gone before. In Jerusalem one might realize a place in the whole Christian church on earth. Travel as pilgrimage is a metaphor for worship, and worship is the way of life for God's people.

As worship in a church that is not one's own would be incomplete without greeting some representative of the custodial congregation of that place, a pilgrimage to Jerusalem would be incomplete without some recognition of the actual residents of the city—Jews, Muslims, and Christians. This extra effort would keep one's pilgrimage grounded in the city. Christian pilgrims in Jerusalem might make special effort to acknowledge Palestinian Christians who, Rosemary Radford Ruether writes, "have remained steadfast in their faith and their land under thirteen centuries of Islamic rule and almost fifty years of Israeli rule."[11] The pilgrim should find time for focused attention to the present suffering of Palestinian and Israeli people. A pilgrimage that floats above the ground in a spiritual fog might not be worship or ritual return at all. It might be a charade and a disgrace, and untrue to the embodied nature of the faith we have received.

Staying at Home

Pilgrimage to Jerusalem is not now and never has been universally recommended or supported by Christian leaders. In an essay entitled "Jerusalem in Song and Psalm," Mordecai S.

Chertoff sketches the ambivalence of Christian teachers toward pilgrimage to Jerusalem and contrasts their indifference and opposition with an unambiguous "attraction to Jerusalem on the part of Jews and Judaism."[12] Augustine, John Chrysostom, Jerome, Luther, and Calvin all opposed pilgrimage to the holy city of Jerusalem (and to other holy cities, such as Rome) for similar reasons: to varying degrees they all held the view that a change of physical place does not effect one's redemption. For example, Jerome taught that "the heavenly sanctuary is open from Britain no less than from Jerusalem." Luther and the Reformers opposed pilgrimage as a vain work, undertaken to gain God's favor. In spite of these teachings, Christians have traveled to the Holy Land, and to Jerusalem, following mental maps drawn for them through familiar scripture and tradition and rediscovering their spiritual home in the city.

Norman Macleod (1812–1872), Queen Victoria's chaplain and a pilgrim to Jerusalem, was one of many in the last half of the nineteenth century who recorded impressions of journeys to the Middle East.[13] In a chapter devoted to Macleod, R. D. Kernohan writes that

in Jerusalem . . . the pilgrim inevitably encounters the full range of impressions, emotions, and tensions provoked by the way Christian claims about eternity related to events of time and place. It is usually the experience of going up to Jerusalem that completes and sums up every pilgrim's progress to the Holy Land. It is also where he may be most aware of the contrast between everyday experiences among the life of a strange city and the extraordinary things—"almost too wonderful to be," as one Christian hymn puts it—that are associated with the history of the place as well as the eschatological visions of Zion.[14]

In Jerusalem impossible layers of history are piled one on another, each one still making a breathing claim on the city. Eastern ways of life, bewildering divisions among Christian communities, heated currents in the present political atmosphere all bear on the visitor to Jerusalem. The Christian pilgrim should be challenged to absorb as much of the current incarnation as possible while discovering dimensions of the city—perhaps not even at the traditional sites—that feed and inform the *impressions, emotions,* and *tensions* of his or her faith and life.

In *The Nature of Doctrine,* George Lindbeck recommends a postliberal strategy of "absorbing the universe into the biblical world."[15] Lindbeck is concerned for doctrine and practice and is not advocating pilgrimage. However, his notions that "religion instantiated in Scripture ... defines being, truth, goodness, and beauty," and that "it is the text, so to speak, which absorbs the world, rather than the world the text"[16] may have implications for the ritual return of the Christian pilgrim to Jerusalem. Through such a journey a Christian pilgrim may be more at home in the city of God and therefore more at home in God's world.

John Tleel, a resident of Jerusalem, describes the power of the city in language that sounds liturgical. As the new Jerusalem constructed through the liturgy contains for a Christian the presence, and therefore the gifts of God, so Jerusalem, destroyed and rebuilt again and again, ritually walked through

by countless pious and impious human beings, offers trans-
forming power to those who enter it:

> Even outside the Old City walls you can sense what
> no other city can give you. . . . Along its narrow
> streets you begin to feel its force. You are changed
> by its shrines and holy places, you are baptized into
> Jerusalem.[17]

As, according to Lindbeck, the theologian should absorb the
world into the biblical idiom, with all its contradictions and
difficulties, the pilgrim to Jerusalem for a few hours or days
might allow his own life to be absorbed into the life of the city.
The intellectual and spiritual posture of such a visitor to the
city would be open and generous, humble and curious, having been informed by scripture and tradition to a gracious
outlook.

The pilgrim should not expect to admire every shrine and
alley. He should not pretend to see beauty in unsightly displays that exhibit nothing more than neglect and cynicism.
Dissonance of many kinds fills the senses in Jerusalem, and
a pilgrimage there is not a trip to a religious theme park. The
beauty of the city is not uniform on the surface of things.
Pilgrimage requires preparation, followed by creative "work"
to build the city and to find one's place there, especially with
those who suffer. The worshiping community, doing God's
work, will not turn away from the poor and disenfranchised.
The work of building the city of God, in liturgy and pilgrimage, is to provide a home for all of God's children, especially
for those with no one to take them in at night, and those in

exile so far away from the city that its lights barely shine even in their memories.

Jerusalem as Home to God's People

The language of our liturgy, the syntax of scripture alive in a local assembly, reveals that we are a restless people, uneasy in our places on earth. We are bothered by the state of human affairs, and we believe that matters could be otherwise. Indeed we believe that matters *are* otherwise. So we pray for God's redemption in our experience, and we work out plans, together and on our own, that justice and peace might be established in our vicinities. As we live together in trust and hope in Christian congregations we thirst for representations of our spiritual templates. We need language and action that symbolize—for personal well-being and for the public health—our most deeply implanted hopes.

Gordon Lathrop describes the present "aching need of the times for an authentic and reliable public symbolism," in other words, the need for a system of meaning with power to orient the life of the individuals in a community. He speaks for the Christian assembly but is aware that such a need is shared "with many people besides Christians." The fundamental task he sets before us is that of juxtaposing classical symbols and current states of affairs, and of describing the resultant meanings. He is interested in communities as they "set ancient symbols carefully yet critically next to current and social realities." Such activity might generate energy and passion and elicit deep human responses.[18]

Setting ancient symbols carefully and critically next to current social realities might well describe the intellectual and psychological tasks before the modern religious pilgrim to Jerusalem. Equipped with his own spiritual map of the place, he will find his mental images challenged. These challenges are opportunities for a number of worthwhile exercises, among these being spiritual reflection, historical correction, cross-cultural engagement, ecumenical dialogue, interreligious encounter, and so on. The modern religious pilgrim might find his Sunday piety strained by current political strife, but a strong living faith should bear the contradictions of, for example, geopolitics, conflicting nationalisms, local prejudices, and secular indifference. These have always been present. They are the choruses and alarms of God's children. They must be faced and engaged by the faithful workers of God.

An Eschatological Place

In a 1994 essay entitled "Christianity in the Third Millennium," Jürgen Moltmann offers a theological vision for world Christianity, trained on Jerusalem:

> Ecclesiastical Eurocentrism is ripe for life in a museum, since the great mass of Christians in the year 2000 will not even live in Europe but outside of it. Without decentralization it won't be possible to achieve a new blossoming of Christianity. We do not need a new center and a new hierarchy but a worldwide covenant of free and equal churches, congregations and Christians. Then we will be able to see our common origin once again. The Christian center on earth is not to be found in Rome, Byzantium, or Geneva but in Jerusalem. We will look to Jerusalem

with the vision of a remembered hope for the original
and final fellowship of Christians from every nation
with the Jews.[19]

This vivid view fits well with the broadest patterns of human
life streaming up perforce to Jerusalem.
Mitri Raheb, a Palestinian Christian, is pastor of the
Evangelical Lutheran Church in Bethlehem. His family has
lived in Bethlehem for hundreds of years. When he writes of
his hope for peace in his native land his words sound like the
culminating reflections at the end of a long spiritual pilgrimage, the realization of a ritual return to the provisional homes
of Jews, Christians, and Muslims in Jerusalem:

> The Jerusalem of which I dream no longer has an
> Almond Tree Gate to separate the east and the west
> sides. It is an open city, large enough to take both
> peoples under its wing. Its small streets and thor-
> oughfares are broad enough to carry adherents of
> all three monotheistic religions and persons of all
> nations. It will be a city about which the Psalmist said,
> "the tribes go up to it" (Ps 122:3) . . . for I am about
> to create Jerusalem as a joy. . . . I have a dream about
> two peoples in whom one can see the cradle of three
> monotheistic religions. It can be seen not only in the
> ancient stones of the Wailing Wall, of the Church
> of the Resurrection, and of the Dome of the Rock,
> but in the people themselves—Jews, Christians, and
> Muslims. A bit of the divinity of their God is evi-
> denced in their dealings with each other, in the way
> they use the freedom and power granted to them.[20]

Visionaries rest longing eyes on Jerusalem, the ancient and renewed city. Jerusalem is so deeply etched in maps—or in name alone—inside Christian hearts that it stands as the chief emblem and destination, hours away by plane, nearby as the Holy Communion of the local assembled congregation. Jerusalem is the place where Christians

> look for the resurrection of the dead,
> and the life of the world to come.

Jerusalem represents the hope inside the Christian faith. The city in its present historical manifestation may remind the informed pilgrim that faith has real reference in time and place, marked by contradictions and conflicts but still alive and longing for peaceful homecoming. The mapping and home building, with reference to Jerusalem, are tedious and time-consuming. Periods of discomfort accompany the work. In the last decade of the eighteenth century Abraham Kalisker warned Jews who planned a move to Jerusalem that the transition might take time, but that they would be transformed:

> Many, many changes and events, experiences and
> fates befall every single man who comes to this land,
> until he adjusts to it, has joy in its stones, and loves its
> dust, until the ruins of the Land of Israel are dearer to
> him than a palace abroad, and dry bread in that place
> dearer than all delicacies elsewhere. But this does not
> happen in one day nor in two, not in a month and not
> in a year. Many a year passes before his initiation is
> over, his initiation into the true life.[21]

In time, Jerusalem would take the travelers in. Some day, following the ritual returns of generation after generation, following countless pilgrim passages and un-numbered prayers, following repeated acts of violence and even unspeakable nighttime horrors on the streets of the city, Jerusalem, shining with the best human hope, representing the highest dreams we have, might open its gates to all.

⇒ NOTES

Introduction: A Place of One's Own

1. Yi-Fu Tuan, *Topophilia: A Study of Environmental Perception, Attitudes and Values* (Englewood Cliffs, New Jersey: Prentice-Hall, Inc., 1974), xiv.

2. Tuan, 247.

3. Gaston Bachelard, *The Poetics of Space* (Boston: Beacon Press, 1969), 172.

4. W. H. Auden, *Collected Poems* (New York: Vintage Books, 1991), 624.

5. Exodus 33:7–11.

One: The Manger

1. Gaston Bachelard, *The Poetics of Space* (Boston: Beacon Press, 1969), 133.

2. Alan Filreis, *Wallace Stevens and the Actual World* (Princeton: Princeton University Press, 1991), 151.

3. Ibid., 154.

4. Frank Kermode, *Wallace Stevens* (New York: Grove Press, Inc., 1960), 24.

5. Wallace Stevens, *The Collected Poems* (New York: Vintage Books, 1990), 76.

6. Stevens used the word *fictive* in describing his work. Throughout his career he made poetic assumptions and claims about the relation of historical conditions—what he knew as the "actual world"
represented in the day's news—and the reflection of his interior life,
or his imagination.

7. Ibid., 12.

8. Ray L. Hart, "The Poiesis of Place," reprinted from *The Journal
of Religion*, Vol. 53, No. 1, January 1973.

9. Ibid., 38.

10. Stevens, 209.

11. Richard Horsley, *The Liberation of Christmas* (New York:
Continuum, 1993), 105.

12. Ibid., 105ff.

13. Vassar Miller, *If I Had Wheels or Love* (Dallas: Southern
Methodist University Press, 1991), 51.

14. Miller, 11.

15. Mark Kidger, *The Star of Bethlehem: An Astronomer's View*
(Princeton: Princeton University Press, 1999), 166ff.

16. Edmund Hoade, OFM, *Guide to the Holy Land* (Jerusalem:
Franciscan Printing Press, 1984), 375 ff.

Two: The Stable

1. Gaston Bachelard, *The Poetics of Space* (Boston: Beacon
Press, 1969), 6–7.

2. Richard Wilbur, *New and Collected Poems* (New York:
Harcourt, 1988), 225.

3. Heinrich Wölfflin, *The Art of Albrecht Dürer* (London: Phaidon
Press, 1971), 127.

4. See Isaiah 44 and Revelation 1.

5. Wilbur, 225.

6. Bruce J. Malina and Richard L. Rohrbaugh, *Social-Science
Commentary on the Synoptic Gospels* (Minneapolis: Fortress Press,
1992), 296.

7. Bachelard, 31.

8. Bachelard, 30.

9. Bachelard, 32.

10. See *Architecture Boston*, November/December 2003, 31ff.

11. Mark 9, Matthew 17, Luke 9.

12. *Built on a Rock*, by Nikolai F. S. Grundtvig, 1783–1872.

13. "The Death of the Hired Man" was originally published in Robert Frost's 1915 collection *North of Boston*. It is widely anthologized and available in several editions of Frost's poems.

14. See Martin Luther's *Large Catechism*.

15. Roland Bainton, *Here I Stand: A Life of Martin Luther* (New York: Mentor Press, 1955), 277–278.

16. *Good Christian Friends, Rejoice.*

17. Genesis 8.

18. Leviticus 12.

19. Mark 1, Matthew 3, Luke 3, and John 1.

20. Jeremy Wood, *The Nativity: Themes in Art* (London: Scala Publications Ltd., 1992), 10.

21. Vassar Miller, *If I Had Wheels or Love* (Dallas: Southern Methodist Press, 1991), 222.

22. Miller, 116.

23. Helen Gardner, editor, *The Metaphysical Poets* (London: Penguin Books, 1972), 39.

24. David Brendan Hopes, *The Glacier's Daughters* (Amherst: University of Massachusetts Press, 1981), 57.

25. Quoted in Simon Schama, *Landscape and Memory* (New York: Alfred A. Knopf, 1995), 244.

26. Bachelard, 109.

Three: Bethlehem

1. Deborah Tall, "Making Peace with Space and Place" in *Rooted in the Land: Essays on Community and Place*, William Vitek and Wes Jackson, eds. (New Haven: Yale University Press, 1996), 106ff.

2. Quoted in *Listening for God, Volume 3*, Paula Carlson and Peter Hawkins, eds. (Minneapolis: Augsburg Fortress, 1994), 104.

3. Yi-Fu Tuan, *Topophilia: A Study of Environmental Perception, Attitudes, and Values* (New York: Columbia University Press, 1974), 193.

4. Robert Bellah et al., *Habits of the Heart: Individualism and Commitment in American Life* (Berkeley: University of California Press, 1985), 282.

5. Yi-Fu Tuan, 101.

6. Richard Davies et al., eds., *A Place Called Home: Writings on the Midwestern Small Town* (St. Paul: Borealis Books, 2003), 8.

7. Frank Conroy, *Dogs Bark, but the Caravan Rolls On: Observations Now and Then* (Boston: Houghton Mifflin Company, 2002), 48.

8. Ibid., 50.

9. Carol Bly, "Quietly Thinking Over Things at Christmas," quoted in Davies, 323ff.

10. Gaston Bachelard, *The Poetics of Space* (Boston: Beacon Press, 1969), 32f.

11. *Image: A Journal of the Arts and Religion,* Number 12, Winter 1995–96, 55.

Four: Mary

1. For a summary of the historical questions surrounding the ancestry of Jesus, see Raymond E. Brown, *The Birth of the Messiah* (New York: Doubleday, 1977).

2. *This Far by Faith: An African American Resource for Worship* (Minneapolis: Augsburg Fortress, 1999).

3. Wendell Berry, *The Country of Marriage* (New York: Harcourt Brace Jovanovich, 1973), 17.

4. From the hymn *Von Himmel Hoch,* text by Martin Luther (1483–1546).

5. William Carlos Williams, *The Collected Poems of William Carlos Williams, 1939–1962, vol. II* (New York: New Directions Publishing Corporation, 2005), 430.

6. I refer to the song "Ghost Riders in the Sky," words and music

by Stan Jones, which has been recorded by Gene Autry, Vaughn Monroe, Peggy Lee, Bing Crosby, Burl Ives, Johnny Cash, and many others.

7. Gerald Stern, *This Time: New and Selected Poems* (New York: W.W. Norton, 1998), 103.

8. Edward Hodnett, editor, *Poems to Read Aloud* (New York: W.W. Norton, 1957), 27.

Five: Jerusalem

1. Elie Wiesel, *A Jew Today* (New York: Vintage Books, 1978), 24–25.

2. Ibid., 29.

3. Jonathan Z. Smith, "Jerusalem: The City as Place," in *Civitas*, Peter Hawkins, ed. (Atlanta: Scholars Press, 1986), 26–38.

4. Ibid., 25.

5. Ibid., 27.

6. Cf. Chronicles 28:11–19.

7. Here Smith draws on the work of Peter Gould, *On Mental Maps* (Ann Arbor: University of Michigan, 1966).

8. Smith, 26.

9. Lutheran Book of Worship, Holy Communion.

10. Robert R. Wilson, "The City in the Old Testament," in *Civitas*, Peter Hawkins, ed. (Atlanta: Scholars Press, 1986), 6.

11. Mitri Raheb, *I Am a Palestinian Christian* (Minneapolis: Fortress Press, 1995), vii.

12. Mordecai S. Chertoff, "Jerusalem in Song and Psalm," in *Jerusalem, City of the Ages*, Alice L. Eckardt, ed. (London: University Press of America, 1987), 226 ff.

13. One estimate is that during this period there was an annual average of forty books on Holy Land travel published in Britain. Norman Macleod's impressions were serialized under the title of *Eastward* in a London magazine, *Good Words*.

14. R. D. Kernohan, *The Road to Zion: Travellers to Palestine and the Land of Israel* (Grand Rapids: Wm. B. Eerdmans, 1995), 53.

15. George A. Lindbeck, *The Nature of Doctrine, Religion and Theology in a Postliberal Age* (Philadelphia: Westminster Press, 1984), 135.

16. Ibid., 118.

17. John N. Tleel, "My Jerusalem," in *Jerusalem: City of the Ages,* Alice L. Eckardt, ed. (London: University Press of America, 1987), 308ff.

18. Gordon Lathrop, *Holy Things, A Liturgical Theology* (Minneapolis: Augsburg Fortress, 1993), 4.

19. Jürgen Moltmann, "Christianity in the Third Millennium," in *Theology Today,* Vol. 51, No. 1 (1994).

20. Raheb, 113–115.

21. Peters, 525.